D1239776

To Dr. John Markley
— In appreciation

Battle Wounds of Iwo Jima

Dr. Tom Brown
Hg. 2-27
5th Mar Div

Semper Fi!

Battle Wounds of Iwo Jima

Thomas M. Brown, M.D.

VANTAGE PRESS
New York

Cover design by Susan Thomas

FIRST EDITION

Copyright © 2002 by Thomas M. Brown, M.D.

Published by Vantage Press, Inc.
516 West 34th Street, New York, New York 10001

Manufactured in the United States of America
ISBN: 0-533-14086-2

Library of Congress Catalog Card No.: 01-130965

0 9 8 7 6 5 4 3 2

This work is dedicated to the memory of Mary Adeline Marsalis Brown, whose prayers, faith, hope, and love sustained me throughout the long seventeen months of duty overseas. Her endearing letters, memories of her delightful smiles, whispers, and devotion cheered me through the catastrophic, thirty-six terrifying days of battle on Iwo Jima. Good soldier that she was, without a whimper she made her singular way through months of gestation to bring forth our first-born midway through that savage struggle, not knowing whether or not I still survived.

Like many a war bride and mother, she sensed her returning warrior was not the same light-hearted gallant she married. She graciously accepted his changes, for better or for worse, the witnessing of such horrible destruction and death in battle about him imposed on her frail hero. With quiet determination she set about to restore both of us to the better wholesome life we both envisioned in those idyllic days prior to that wrenching departure we, like thousands of others, experienced in those dark, early morning hours at San Diego as we headed out for the unknown.

Contents

Foreword

It was my very good fortune and honor to serve as commanding officer of the Second Battalion, Twenty-seventh Marines, at the battle for Iwo Jima. A commander is only as good as the men who support him. The officers and men of that battalion were as fine as any commander could desire. Lt. j.g. Tom Brown was a member of that group as an assistant battalion surgeon. His performance was considerate and exceptional. We were fortunate to have a service doctor of his caliber as a member of our battalion.

His thorough, capable training of the corpsmen and litter bearers was plainly evident in the Iwo Jima operation, especially in their efficient handling of the unexpectedly large volume of casualties. His men had the utmost confidence in him and were indoctrinated with a tireless enthusiasm in their work and pride in their accomplishments in caring for the wounded.

Lieutenant junior grade Brown was painfully wounded on March 4, 1945, and was evacuated to the Fifth Marine Division Hospital. He refused to be further evacuated from there and returned to his work in our aid station. There he continued his ministrations to the wounded. His service in connection with operation against the enemy from February 19 through March 26, 1945, was meritorious. His conduct throughout the battle was in keeping with the highest traditions of the United States Naval Service.

—Brig. Gen. John W. Antonelli, USMC (Ret.)

Preface: Overview of the Battle of Iwo Jima

The island battles of the Pacific in World War II were much like cockfights. The two contestants were turned loose in small arenas to go at each other in intense fury. All available weapons and wits were used to thrust and claw at each other. Like cockfights, those island battles ended because one of the participants was mortally wounded. It had so little left of personnel, food, water, ammunition, and weapons, all necessary to sustain fighting. The second fighter was less wounded.

Iwo Jima, or "Sulfur Island," an island 2.5 miles wide at its greatest dimension and less than 5.5 miles at its longest, contained less than 8 square miles of landmass within its irregular coastline. Sulfur Island was so named because of the great abundance of that nonmetallic free chemical found within its soil. Prior to World War II, the Japanese, who owned it, mined sulfur commercially at the island. GIs nicknamed it Pork Chop Island because of its graphic similarity to that porcine cut. At the very narrow, south end stands the top of an extinct volcano, Mount Suribachi. At the time of the assault its height was 550 feet. Following its capture, it was truncated by bulldozers and other earth-moving equipment to render the angle of landing less acute and safer for incoming planes approaching from the south. In the widest portion of that small landmass, cliffs extend laterally to each coast like wings of some giant bird reaching outward beyond a narrow tail, which slopes down into the ocean at each side. To the north of the cliffs in that island's broad midsection are two lesser peaks designated by strategists as Hill #362A and Hill #382. These also may be the tips of extinct volcanoes, which contributed to the formation of Iwo Jima. A line drawn straight between those two peaks and extending to the east and west coast approximates the greatest width of the island. Most of Airstrip #2 lay to the south of such an imaginary line, and all of Airstrip #3 lay to the north of it. Unfinished Airfields #2 and #3 were respectively more or less to the south and north of these two peaks at the day of the assault.

In that wide portion, the soil is much firmer. Scattered over it are craggy groups of volcanic rocks of varying sizes. Many of these serve as vents for steam and fumes rising from deep in the earth and passing on through them to the surface, from where they drift about in breezes swirling above. The small clouds of steam often bore the repulsive odor of sulfur dioxide, much like the stench of rotten eggs. During battle, U.S. troops often used such vents to warm cans of rations in the heat and steam.

On February 19, 1945, more than 30,000 U.S. troops landed on the southern portion of the east coast in an armed assault against more than 21,000 Sons of the Empire of the Rising Sun to capture the island fortress. For the most part, the defenders were sincerely dedicated to dying, if necessary, for a supposedly divine emperor.

Several months prior, in June 1944, Saipan and other Marianas islands were captured by troops of the U.S. Army and Marines. Immediately afterward construction of many large airfields was begun on Saipan, Tinian, and Guam. From these, great flights of our B-29 bombers flew to attack Tokyo and other large industrial and military targets in Japan proper. Many of our aircraft in these flights were badly damaged by the enemy during such attacks and were obliged to ditch into the ocean. Others did so because of exhausted fuel supplies.

Why was tiny Iwo Jima deemed to be of great strategic importance at this time? First, because of its finished airfield, which was already functional, and because of the two unfinished, which quickly could be rendered operable. Iwo Jima could be made into a safe haven for impaired aircraft and their personnel unable to return all that fourteen-hundred-mile flight to the Marianas. A second and just as important reason was the substantial radar facility installed there by the Japanese. Iwo Jima is located roughly halfway between Tokyo and Saipan, about seven hundred miles from each. That radar facility had the capacity to pick up radar signals from the huge fleets of bombers before they flew as far north as Iwo. The radar personnel then radioed Tokyo over two hours ahead of time, before the bombers reached their targets. This enabled the defenders to make adjustments in their antiaircraft sightings, to send fighter planes aloft more than two hours before the B-29s reached their targets, and to sound air-raid warnings to alert all personnel to seek shelter. Eradication of the radar facility was imperative. A third reason for the seizure of Iwo Jima was that the airstrips on it would permit stationing of fighter groups on the island. These could afford added protection for the bombers as they flew in the zone between Iwo and the mainland targets seven hundred miles to the north.

Our strategic planning, preparation for logistical activities, and preliminary training intensified after the fall of Saipan. The newly commissioned Fifth Marine Division plunged into preparation for its spearhead attack in early 1944 at Camp Pendleton, near the huge port at San Diego. Following its participation in the capture of the Marianas, the Fourth Marine Division launched into its training program in its camp in a desert on the island of Maui in the Hawaiian Islands; and the Third Marine Division on the island of Guam, also in the Marianas.

Seasoned campaigners of special U.S. Marine forces, the Paratroopers and the Raiders, returned from battles in the Solomon Islands to enjoy thirty-day leaves back home in the States. Paratroopers were a force of especially trained tough combat soldiers who prepared to make parachute jumps in attacks behind enemy lines or wherever needed. Such jumps were never needed in those Solomon Island fights. They participated in amphibious attacks only. The Paratroopers were then disbanded. When they returned from their leaves, many of them were assigned positions of leadership in the Fifth Division units to provide stability and experience for the unseasoned recruits. Raiders were commando-type special forces that landed behind enemy lines or found other pathways to such positions in surprise raids. They also provided experience and a stabilizing influence among unseasoned troops in their combat training.

As an unseasoned battalion surgeon, I was much impressed by the appearance of these special troops assigned to our unit when they reported into Sick Bay for their routine physical examinations required for new personnel. Their skins were still deeply browned from their long exposure to subtropical rays of sunlight. They were gaunt and hollow-eyed. The whites of their eyes were very yellow in color due to Atabrine, the antimalarial drug that they self-administered daily for long months in the Solomon Islands to prevent infestation by the parasites of the disease transmitted by the mosquitoes of the jungles in which they fought. They appeared much aged beyond their youthful years.

At the other point of rivalry, it was a foregone conclusion of Japanese strategists that the military installation at Iwo Jima, with its established airfields, would be targeted by the U.S. planners for the next advance. Some officers in the higher echelons of Japanese military organizations were opposed to the initial attack against the United States at Pearl Harbor. They were, nevertheless, true to their cause and devoted their great expertise to the fortification of Iwo Jima. Seasoned veterans of battles in Manchuria and along the eastern coast of China were transferred to Iwo to reinforce unseasoned troops already there. Long before 1945, the best mining engineers of the Japanese army were brought there to design a system of communicating caves, tunnels, blockhouses, bunkers, spider traps, ramparts, and firing trenches. A sizable body of civilians was shipped there to complement troops in the construction of twenty-five miles of tunnels dug through volcanic soil. The civilians were shipped back before the Americans ever landed. In one segment of this magnificent underground system there were seven stories of tunnels. Either the extent of these tunnels or their military impact or both were unperceived by the U.S. intelligence prior to battle.

Large and small cannons, huge and smaller mortars, and anti-aircraft were critically and protectively placed by the Japanese to resist attack. Great numbers of machine guns were installed in blockhouses and bunkers in such intricacy that every square foot of the flat surfaces of island facing the coastal approaches was registered for cross-fire coverage and mutual support. Every soldier had his assignment for the hour of attack. These installations were so deeply dug, so well encased in concrete, and so well concealed that weeks and weeks of bombing by the U.S. Air Forces did little damage to them and their personnel. Three days of shelling by sixteen-inch cannons of our great battleships far out at sea did little to alter the potentials of these installations. Artillery and large mortars were emplaced in caves to be run out and fired only as needed. They were not generally exposed to all that preinvasion bombardment and shelling; nor did they suffer destructive effects. Enemy forces on the land surfaces fled at the first sound of air-raid alarms or the first bright flashes of cannon fire from those battleships so far out at sea. They fled into those various underground installations. There they remained safely ensconced. It was business as usual as they continued to move supplies and personnel about inside the concealments in that formidable subterranean maze of the fortress until the all-clear signals were sounded. When the day of our assault did arrive, they were ready and waiting. Their mission was to inflict all damage possible and to delay as much as possible when preparation for the final great day of defense of the homeland should arrive.

When the U.S. Marines came, the Japanese were incredibly difficult to spot in their spider traps, caves, and tunnels. In more open positions, they knelt behind camouflaged ramparts of dirt, stone, boards, and logs. The most obvious identifications of positions were flashes of gunfire. These lasted for a brief moment only and were not always perceived accurately. The die was cast. Even though the Marines could not rapidly identify the hidden locations, they courageously went at the fire from the open beaches of the east coast. The Fifth Marine Division fanned out as it moved in two parallel lines across a narrow half-mile of land between the sandy beaches of the east coast and the west side. The line on the left was formed by the Twenty-eighth regiment. As it stretched toward the west, the regiment turned south to begin a bitter fight to capture that five-hundred-foot hill, Mount Suribachi. The Twenty-seventh turned right and northward toward a wall of high cliffs that stretched laterally like two great wings from a central body, spreading east and west from a flat plateau, which extended much further in the direction of the north shore and expanded in all directions. The Marines were unprotected except for their foxholes, some deep craters where the sixteen-inch shells from the battleships had exploded, and the high southern embankments of Airfield #1. Otherwise our boys were easy targets for the Japanese.

Intelligence was unaware of the myriad of tunnels that had been built by the Japanese and thus told our commanding officers that the capture of Iwo would require only three or four days. How wrong they were. Iwo was one of the bloodiest battles fought in World War II. The Marines moved forward against twenty-one thousand pairs of unseen eyes, which monitored every visible move. Except for the Marines' own covering fire, they were unprotected from snipers and bunker-concealed machine guns. Unexpected grenades were rolled and hurled down at them from Suribachi. From the cliffs to the north, as well as from the slopes of that hill on the south, the Marines were under the constant, withering fire of mortars, machine guns, cannons, and rockets of all sizes. Slowly, steadily forward they went despite the constant surveillance and counterattacks. Their choices were few: move on, stay put and be ground to hamburger by the intense enemy fire, or retreat to the beaches from where they had started. They were never trained to retreat.

Contributors

Corpsmen: *Roy H. Brown, Edward R. Jones* and *Gerald Cunningham:* Hitting The Beach
Edward R. Jones: his battlefield snapshots
Lester J. Murrah: soliloquies
Ed Jones, Paul Bradford, and *Glen Lougee:* for their epilogues

Marines: *Mike Ladich, Dick Tilghman, Allan Mortenson, Lelon Young, Wallace Shaklee, Lou Balog, Bill Bainter, Jay Rebstock, Leonard Nederveld, Chuck Allman, Austin Montgomery,* who contributed their soliloquies of Death Valley

Acknowledgments

Angela and Dwayne Morris: for their patience and for their many
hours of editing, advising, and organizing

Steven C. Brown: for editing, advice, and suggestions in styling

Col. John H. Lauck, USMC (ret.) military advisor

And especially to Col. Billy Menges, USMC (ret.) for his gracious
permission to use his *Memoirs of Iwo Jima* without restriction.

Introduction

My first recalled exposure to the medical profession occurred in the summer of 1920 while we were visiting our Grandmother Lucas and Aunt Nell Hannah in Hamersville, Ohio. One might say a relationship was established as a result of being rear-ended. At the age of little more than three and a half years, while exploring an old-fashioned chain-driven well pump mounted on a concrete slab, which encased the well below, my unsuspecting little feet tripped over some unperceived object, precipitating a sitting-posture descent onto a broken milk bottle on the slab. From there, someone with strong arms hustled me across the gravel highway to the office of kindly Dr. Roush. That scene of his skills is still clearly remembered. Sitting in his ample captain's chair, he laid me sunny side up across his thighs and began deftly removing bits of splintered glass from my bloody rump. Those shelves of huge brown bottles of pills and powders on the wall to his left gripped my fancy in such great interest and concentration, not a wail was heard.

Three years before my admission to Indiana University School of Medicine and shortly after our mother's death caused by cancer of the lung due to secondhand Bull Durham tobacco smoke, my brother, Lee, and I concluded we should and would go to medical school. Poverty of the Great Depression was inconvenient and unappealing. Meanwhile, our father died abruptly of a second heart attack. Having absolutely no perception of how we might meet the financial needs of medical school, Lee and I naively, injudiciously, ignorantly, and persistently plodded on. Somehow we cleared the scholastic and financial bars.

Actually, the early days of education of the author paralleled the terroristic moves of the Nazi Party getting under way in Germany and those, also, of the dominant political and military forces of the Japanese being exercised in China. During our high school years, rumblings of volcanic political activity in Germany and Italy began to appear in local newspapers. The adult populace of United States, soured by the post–World War I turn of international events in Europe, had become isolationist. The great sacrifices of death and maiming among our troops in World War I, plus the inability of the European allies to emerge with a satisfactory, enduring peace afterward, left the United States cynical with regard to international politics. As Mussolini and Hitler were elevated to positions of greater eminence in their own governments, we stayed at greater than arm's length. Why should we Americans become involved if the European Alliance was unable to manage its own households?

At 10:00 A.M., on December 8, 1941, the junior class at the Indiana University School of Medicine ceased its frenetic chatter about the historic events of the day before. The heavyset, highly respected, sober-faced professor of surgery Dr. Jacob Berman lumbered into the lecture room to begin his usual Monday-morning presentation on an appropriate subject. He slowly, silently scanned the expectant group of students in the seats before him, hesitated, let his gaze wander to whatever unpleasant view met him from beyond the classroom window, and instructed us, "Gentlemen, stay in your seats. This will be a long war. Riflemen are in good supply. Doctors will be scarce. Finish your formal medical education. This will be a long war. You will get your chance. I know. I was in the same situation twenty-five years ago." He was a prophet as well as a surgeon.

Our senior year was shortened two months. We attended school without interruption throughout 1942 and graduated in late

December. Two weeks after Pearl Harbor, some of us applied for Ensign commissions in the U.S. Navy. Some older student told us it was the best service. Two months later we received notice of our commissions, which were issued to us on an inactive basis. In my application for the commission was a statement instructing the applicant to place a check mark in his choice of three or four available types of duties as a medical officer. Being surfeit with noble thoughts of service to my nation, I checked the one for "Any Duty Land or Sea." In its omniscient understanding of my desire, my government gave me exactly that duty.

Thus jogged my path in a tortuous medical career. Along with eighteen or twenty other Marines in the third assault wave, I was crowded into one of those noisy all-metal Landing Vehicles, Tractors (LVTs), those wonderful unsung all-purpose, amphibious transports, churning into the battle before us on Red Beach One. While I was cruising through high school and college, war was never on the agendas of my dreams for my future. Other than to fulfill my duty in caring for the wounded in all the explosions, smoke, dust, and dither ahead of us, I was not quite sure how I should or would conduct myself in those early minutes after hitting the beach or in the days to follow. We were part of "the Greatest Generation." We didn't realize it until Tom Brokaw told us fifty-five years later.

Battle Wounds of Iwo Jima

Part I

The Wounding

1

Voyage to Death Valley

By the time all the troops of Second Battalion, Twenty-seventh Marines, the ancillary troops, ammunition, weapons, and other miscellaneous supplies were loaded aboard Troopship 119, also named the USS *Highlands,* to begin the fateful trip to Saipan, January 1945 was almost spent. After hoisting anchor at the port of Hilo, Hawaii, it sailed to the great U.S. Navy port Pearl Harbor at the island of Oahu, Territory of Hawaii. There more supplies of assorted kinds were loaded on various ships of a convoy and staff meetings at various levels of the Fifth Amphibious Corps were conducted in preparation for battle. Operations officers dispensed sealed orders of commands to be opened for further instructions while at sea. The USS *Highlands* lay in port for three days, becoming, during that time, a small part of a huge convoy of ships transporting the Fourth and Fifth Marine Divisions to Eniwetok in the Kwajalein atoll and farther yet to the open port at Saipan in the Marianas Island group located a bit more than 1,400 miles south of Tokyo, Japan. Four days prior to the departure of that large convoy from Pearl Harbor, a smaller, slower convoy containing small vessels transporting the amphibious landing craft headed for the same open port of Saipan. There the assault troops would be transferred to the small ships just prior to leaving Saipan to hit the beach at Iwo.

During those days at Saipan, supplies also were dispensed from larger ships to the smaller ships bearing the amphibious tractors. While the ships were at anchor in port, some of the Marines watched from the topsides of their ships the numerous B-29 bombers returning from runs over Tokyo and other Japanese industrial cities to the many Saipan airstrips. One of the Marines, Pfc. Billy Menges, of Fox Company 2-27 (Second Battalion, Twenty-seventh Regiment), noted his observations of these aircraft in his memoirs written years later for interested relatives and friends. Some of the B-29s landed faultlessly at the ends of return flights. Others landed askew because of faulty gear partially destroyed over those targets by antiaircraft fire or by enemy fighter planes lurking in the distance to protect targets as the bombers approached. Still others crash-landed, either because their fuel supplies were exhausted or because their landing instruments were damaged. Even worse were those so impaired they crashed, exploded, and burned. Many bombers and their crews never returned. They were shot down or else crash-landed at sea because of structural damage or expended fuel supplies. As the Marines watched those many dramatic and tragic landings, they gained a clear-cut knowledge of the necessity of their mission.

2
D-Day

For four days the crews of those smaller LCIs plowed and bounced through more than 700 miles of dark, rough seas toward that small target island. The Marines meanwhile digested the plans of assault and rehearsed the final hours of D-Day, during which they checked weapons and packs and moved on down from quarters to the steel deck below. The LCIs held in their second deck below topside the amphibious tractors, which were loaded as assigned. The same Billy Menges, a rifleman of the First Platoon of Fox Company 2-27, positioned himself in the front of his LVT next to the ramp end. In addition to the pack, weapon, and all other accessories, he was assigned to carry a forty-pound shape charge of explosive ashore and leave it in a tank trap beyond Red Beach One. The ship's ramp at the bow end was lowered at the designated minute. His and other tractors poured from the steel deck out over the ramp, which leaned down to the ocean's surface. Each tractor then moved into a small, circling group. At a given signal they moved into a straight line formation, the first wave of tractors leading the assault. As a flag was lowered to signal their departure, the LVTs revved up their engines and headed in. The crews of the landing vehicles were instructed to head across the beach up over the sandy terrain of the terraces of the beach and on inland two hundred yards before unloading their cargoes of Marines.

In actuality the vehicle in which Menges rode bumped as it hit the beach, churned forward ten yards, and stalled as it hit the ten-foot-high soft, sandy terrace. The LVT ramp was lowered. He was pushed out by other troops behind him and on into the conflict. In moving forward and upward, they were retarded by the soft, shifting sand. Some fell to their knees in it. They helped one another through the sand by forming chains like bucket brigades. The Marines clung to one another and pulled forward. When they got to the top of the slope, the troops stopped. Menges paused to catch his breath again and to clean his rifle, which was covered with sand. His platoon leader, George Piotrowski, stayed with Menges to protect him until the cleaning task was finished. They then wended their way forward through the eerie landscape marked by shell holes and craters everywhere.

As Menges climbed over the edge of the terrace, he stopped a few moments to reconnoiter. He looked back at the beach, where he viewed another wave approaching a few feet offshore just before landing. He then turned his gaze to the left toward Mount Suribachi. An airplane came around the south side of the hill and headed in his direction. Something was wrong. Its machine guns blazed away on friendly areas, and its nose tilted downward. He was dumbfounded by the course it took as it went by. It headed on down and plowed right into the wave of tractors, hitting one broadside and turning it over. A tractor next to it was struck by a wing as the plane swung around on impact with the tractor. A few men were killed by the accident. The plane stayed afloat. Menges could see the pilot, dead in the cockpit and slumped over. He presumably was hit by enemy aircraft and lost control on approaching Mount Suribachi.

Independently Corpsman Glen Lougee, the senior corpsman of Fox Company and also in the first wave, reported seeing a U.S. fighter plane struck by antiaircraft fire as it came around Mount Suribachi. It headed down toward the tractors and struck one of them as it hit the water. He observed it to hit a craft in its midsection. The front and rear ends of the vessel flipped upward.

The two halves immediately plunged vertically below the surface of the sea.

As the Marines moved on over into the tank trap, Menges left his shape charge in it for men following to use on partially destroyed emplacements. Because mortar and artillery fire began to pour in, they were told to move on. Menges told Corp. Jim Moe he could not do so until he had a weapon that worked. Jim nodded understandingly. Again Piotrowski stayed behind until the weapon was usable.

After a few minutes, Billy and George were ready to move forward. By then the terrace was marked with craters and shell holes everywhere. Barbed-wire entanglements, shattered bunkers, and blockhouses were all around. The ground was littered with Japanese bodies. It was like being on the moon or in some other dry, barren landscape. They followed the tracks of members of their company until they found them hunkered down in scrub brush and irregular ground. By then the troops were three hundred yards inland, not quite halfway across the island at its narrowest segment. They were still pounded by incessant mortar and artillery fire as it landed in the sand and exploded, covering them with the sand and dry volcanic ash. Surprisingly, Fox Company suffered very few casualties in that long bombardment.

As they moved on, Menges's squad was on the left side of a tank, which came up to help. After another one hundred yards, he was alerted by other members in the platoon who yelled and pointed in his direction toward a point beyond. The tank moved up on an elevated piece of ground. It was unwittingly sitting right above a large bunker. Menges pulled one of the two rifle grenades from the rings on his pack, pulled the pin, leaned over, and dropped it right down in front of the bunker opening. After it exploded, he pulled the pin of the second one, leaned over the edge, and threw it into the same opening to destroy possible enemies within. The tank moved forward, and the men moved with it. The bunker was left behind to be demolished by troops coming on from the rear. The situation stabilized and quieted. All at once John Tuohey screamed, "Oh, it's hot! It's hot! It stings; it stings!"

Clarence Milburne was standing in place motionless and staring straight ahead. Milburne was stunned, having taken a direct hit by a Japanese bullet at the top of his helmet. It traveled directly between his helmet and its liner and made an exit through the back side of the helmet to career off into Tuohey's back. Tuohey was evacuated. Milburne stayed.

Progress across the rest of the island seemed slow. Eventually, Fox Company was at its target point on the right flank of Easy Company. It made a short right turn toward the north. Thus they successfully severed Mount Suribachi's installations from the rest of the island.

Fox Company spent the next half hour creeping and crawling forward and dashing in short runs. It moved in concert with Easy Company on its left flank and First Battalion, Twenty-seventh, on the right. By now it was 1300, and they were nearing the D-Day objective of 2-27. As they crossed a small cleared area, a large Nambu machine gun fired from the left. Everyone hit the ground. Staff Sergeant Hershberger yelled back, "Who has a rifle grenade?" Menges had two. Hershberger told him, "That fire is from a pillbox about fifty yards over on our left. See if you can get one in there and quiet that guy." Menges yelled back that he needed a minute to prepare. Meanwhile, Sergeant Hershberger informed the rest of the platoon that they were to get up and rush to a line of brush and small trees a short distance away to the front as soon as Menges fired.

He could not see the pillbox from his position on the ground because of a slight rise ahead, so Menges crawled up the rise. He spotted the pillbox. Just beyond the rise in the ground was a deep trench. Menges rolled over into it for a better firing position. He knew the Jap saw him go into the trench and would be waiting for him to expose himself. When he was ready to shoot, he rose quickly, took aim, and fired. The grenade bounced off the mound without detonating. Menges called back to the others to hold up. After moving to another position five yards to the left, he stood and took a little more time to aim. The grenade not only hit the target; it went right through the obvious opening and detonated inside. Smoke poured out in all directions. The platoon was up and running in seconds. It was now 1400. Easy and Fox moved two hundred yards beyond the day's objective and dug foxholes the rest of the day. Food and water were brought from the rear as they prepared for a banzai attack.

Their misery wasn't yet over. Several tanks and trucks came up and parked in the tree line to the rear. They were prime targets. Artillery and mortar fire poured in all night. The tankers and truckers could sleep safely beneath their vehicles, but infantrymen were completely exposed. As D-Day waned, a head count revealed Fox Company had lost twenty men, some killed, more wounded.

Shortly after noon the next day, Easy and Fox Companies moved northward with Dog Company in reserve. Intermittently they crawled slowly, then ran in short, irregular dashes. Safety in movement was tenuous at best, because the long-distance fire from beyond the cliffs to the north produced many casualties in all three companies. Fox Company moved north along a wide dirt pathway, which might have been a road for the Japanese. One of a group of Marine tanks moved up into this road ahead of the infantry, stopped, and lobbed some shells into a mounded area ahead. Menges stepped to the side of the road and on down into a knee-high trench parallel to the dirt pathway. For some unknown reason he experienced a distinct feeling of danger. He glanced off to his left and spied a cleared area, which led to a small mound thirty or forty yards beyond. A short distance ahead of him was a low, small tree stump. He carefully kept the stump between himself and the mound. He had a suspicious feeling about that mound, even though there was no sign of activity in or around it.

After a number of rounds, the accompanying tank stopped firing. Menges's squad leader, Dewey Flinn, gave the word to move up. He stood a few yards behind Menges, who started down the ditch, intending to use it for cover as long as possible. Menges went about fifteen yards farther, which placed him in front of the tank. At that point the ditch took a forty-five-degree turn to the left. He was looking right into the forward firing opening of a concrete bunker covered by dirt. It wasn't more than ten feet away.

Instincts developed in training quickly took over. Menges threw his left leg up and forward and did a barrel roll to the right side and on out of the ditch. He came to a stop almost under a left tank track. He crawled under the tank's guns to the right side of the tank and started to point to the ditch he had just left. At that moment Sergeant Flinn stepped down into the ditch where Menges was a moment before. Flinn's position was disastrous. He remained standing and was a clear shot for a sniper in the mounded spider trap and was shot through the abdomen. Although Flinn was evacuated right away, he later died aboard ship because of those wounds. Other troops swarmed over the spider trap and destroyed it.

3

Into the Valley

Our "Good Old Second Batt" was ordered to move into the area between the northeast end of Airfield #1 and the southwest end of Airfield #2 on D+6 (the sixth day of battle). Dog Company moved in to reinforce positions in the 26th and was not available for the jump-off. Easy Company waited on the left, Fox Company on the right. All morning and well into the afternoon large mortars, artillery, air strikes, and naval gunfire hammered the enemy positions up front. The battleships had left a day or two before and no longer provided their heavy bombardment. Lesser naval cannons were in support. As the hour for the attack on Death Valley neared, Easy Company pivoted ninety degrees in order that Fox Company might move into a position on its left flank and face the valley opening. Ahead, the ground sloped downward into a rather deep indentation in the terrain three hundred yards away. Beyond was a precipitous ridge guarding the high ground on farther north. The immediate objective was a low, sandy pocket. The enemy concealed themselves in the high ground beyond in an arc-shaped defense.

At 1500 both companies jumped off simultaneously, running short distances in semicrouches. Second Platoon of Fox Company was on the left flank. First Platoon was between it and Easy Company. The front line seemed to make rapid progress. Menges was near the end of his platoon as they entered the area marked with small shell holes and many small mounds. When an artillery barrage began, he jumped into a small shell hole alongside Robert Goff to avoid the barrage. Goff was a bazooka man, but his bazooka was filled with sand. He asked Menges to stay with him while he cleaned it. In a few minutes it was operable again. One of those "Whistling Nellies" landed nearby, covering both of them with sand and dust. The platoon moved on ahead as Goff was cleaning his weapon. They started after their comrades following their footprints down the valley. The sound of rifle fire made it easy to locate them. Near the end of the valley they stopped to get their bearings. The valley opened out into a stadium-like bowl, with the high ground and cliffs on the other side. They saw both platoons pinned down in an arc-shaped line to the left front. The two men crept and crawled and made short dashes until they joined the others. In one of those short sprints, Menges almost stumbled over a man. He was Adolph Fang, wounded and bleeding profusely. Adolph, the other bazooka man in the assault squad, had taken five slugs in his chest from a machine gun as he stepped forward to get a shot at a pillbox ten yards to his front.

Sgt. George O'Keefe, who was assisting Adolph, took a bullet in his right eye. Good Catholic that he was, he was saying his rosary, presuming his time had come. (George is still living.) By this time a corpsman had busied himself working on Fang. Someone suggested Menges fire a grenade into the pillbox. He looked about for a satisfactory firing position and found none. The alternative was to move to the left a few yards and get a fix on the target. As he rose upward to look over the edge of the escarpment just ahead, Bill Bainter, a Browning Automatic Rifle man (BAR man) in the squad, was firing into that and other pillboxes beyond. Bainter called, "My God, B.C., be careful! That guy can really shoot!" Jumping up quickly to sight in and fire, Menges was greeted instantly by the sharp spray of sand in his face. The sniper probably saw the top of Menges's helmet coming up as he stood upright. Luckily the round was a little low instead of right between the eyes. He ducked down quickly and took a long, deep, thankful breath.

At that moment, Bob Goff crawled over near Menges and removed his helmet. Several men yelled at him to put it back on his head, but Goff said he could see better without it. As his bazooka cleared the top edge of the escarpment everyone heard that awful *wock* sound. The bullet split the top of his head. As he fell, his brain started oozing out on the ground. He was finished.

Farther to the left was a small clump of bushes with a flat opening underneath one. Menges called to Bainter to keep the guy in the pillbox busy while he crawled over to try for a shot. Just then Corp. Ed Schumaker of the machine-gun platoon moved in with his squad and gun. He suggested he would like to have the spot to set up and fire across the entire front. Reluctantly Menges looked elsewhere. Meanwhile the mortar shells kept dropping in the area accompanied by rifle and machine-gun fire from those Japanese pillboxes.

Easy Company was having a tough time. Tanks were called to bolster the attack. The mortar fire shifted to them, and some were knocked out immediately. Infantrymen nearby were wounded and killed by shrapnel from those same mortar shells. When Corp. Ed Schumaker's crew started shooting, the machine gun raised a lot of dust, as they always did. Assuming the dust came from an enemy position, a tank fired at it. Disaster struck. A 75mm U.S. shell, right on target, hit Schumaker's foot, severing it at the ankle. He crawled out in front of the tank screaming at it to cease fire. Just after that Corpsman Cunningham came around to take care of Ed. An ammunition carrier lay nearby, front side down. Clarence Milburne yelled to the motionless carrier. Getting no response, Clarence crawled over and turned the dead man, who had had his face blown away. As Clarence stared at the mutilated face, he was so shocked at the horrible sight that he began crying and frothing at the mouth. For Milburne, too, the battle was over.

Another machine gunner led him away to the rear. He never returned.

By this time the casualty list was five men killed and thirty-five wounded. They were badly disorganized and in need of replacements, but there were none. Battalion headquarters decided to pull back Fox Company and send Dog Company into the fight. With darkness approaching, withdrawal appeared impossible in all that terrible gunfire. When word was passed to withdraw, Staff Sgt. Jim Gibson of the Second Platoon stood to his feet in front of friend and foe alike so everyone could hear. In his high-pitched voice he announced that each man was to withdraw the same way he came in, back up the valley. He shouted, "Every man who walks out of here will take a wounded comrade along! I will personally shoot anyone who goes out empty-handed!"

The enemy kept firing, but as a miracle from God, Jim stood there like a rock, unharmed, and directed the withdrawal, eventually preventing many more casualties. No one knew why other company officers and noncommisioned officers were not there. Why did that responsibility fall on Jim Gibson alone? He was magnificent in doing what no one else could—the epitome of a brave, dedicated, noble Marine. His hour did not end there. He did much more.

On the way back up the valley, some assisted the walking wounded; others carried the disabled wounded. Someone set up a collecting station at the head of the valley to accommodate the wounded. More tanks came to evacuate them. Adolph Fang lay there on the ground. Mike Ladich and Menges lifted and supported him while he moved toward one of the tanks. As they hoisted him up on the deck of the tank, Adolph asked, "Mike, do you think I'll get the Purple Heart for this?" That remark almost moved Menges to tears. In obvious shock and pain due to the five bullet wounds and not knowing whether he might live or die, Fang still manifested a sense of humor in the face of his tragedy. He survived, and they all keep in contact with one another. Fortunately, George

14

O'Keefe recovered with unimpaired vision in the injured eye. Ed Schumaker lost his leg and remained bitter about that unfortunate incident the rest of his life. Unfortunately, Bob Goff did not survive.

After the wounded and dead were gone, the remainder of Fox Company gathered in a low-lying area surrounded by some empty bunkers and scrubby brush. Gibson returned there and organized a defense formation for the night. No sooner were the Marines settled when Gibson appeared again. He did not know Menges by name but ordered, "Come on, big guy. I need you for a job." In addition to Menges, Gibson recruited ten other guys to go back with him to the battalion supply area, where they were loaded heavily with ammunition, water, and food. Menges struggled along with a dozen bandoliers of M-1 rifle ammo strung around his neck and carrying a five-gallon can of water. All of them were overloaded, stumbling and falling as they went. Gibson kept helping them and pushing them along until they arrived safely back with the company, where they were dismissed to return to their foxholes. It was 2100. All were completely exhausted. Those not on watch fell asleep instantly. For his efforts that day, Jim Gibson was awarded the Bronze Star Medal, one not even close to recognizing his accomplishments. He should have been awarded the Congressional Medal of Honor. He certainly earned it by his courageous actions that day.

So severe was the decimation of 2-27 (Second Battalion, Twenty-seventh Regiment) that it went back in reserve to reorganize and to prepare to reenter the fray. D+8 was special to Bill Menges. Fox Company rejoined other frontline units in another attack up the left side of the island. They achieved moderate gains. Casualties were light. He had a very warm feeling along with a continuous headache throughout the day. They mattered but little. After all that had happened during the week, he had occasion to be happy. He was still alive on the nineteenth anniversary of his birth.

On D+9 the three shot-up companies of 2-27 awakened to behold the approaches of another formidable ridge line. Early that morning, Fifth Division headquarters graciously decided to replace them with elements of the 28th Marines. 2-27 was sent to Corps Reserve back by Mount Suribachi. Actually, that situation did not feature much rest, especially the first night. What a nightmare! Random artillery shells dropped in continually. A gas alarm sounded about 0200 when some of those shells stuck a nearby ammo dump. Scattered rifle fire punctuated the darkness all night as Japanese soldiers previously buried in some of the caves of Mount Suribachi dug their way out and attempted to flee northward through the lines.

For six days the daily chores of 2-27 included mopping up caves and other cracks and crevices in ample supply around the base of Mount Suribachi. Several hundred of the enemy were killed in the numerous caves, leaving but few to be captured in the caves that were sealed with flame throwers and dynamite while in reserve. The ever-present smell of death and burned bodies created all kinds of imaginary horrors. Faint hearts and weak stomachs fared poorly on that detail.

During that break while back at the rear, some did have the opportunity to go to the top of Mount Suribachi and look back over the island and its beaches, as well as to view the vast array of ships still lying offshore. It was an amazing sight: the beaches littered with appalling examples of all kinds of wreckage of war. Sometimes ironic incidents occurred there, especially in the early part of the invasion. Men with relatively minor but disabling wounds were tragically killed while awaiting evacuation to hospital and other ships as the tremendous murderous heavy artillery and mortar fire fell on them at unexpected, inopportune times. Such are the fortunes of war. But by the end of those six days the strength and spirits of most men of 2-27 were almost normal again. Replacement clothing was at a premium. A few men managed to obtain new dungarees, but most were threadbare at the elbows and knees as a result of living on the ground in the abrasive volcanic ash.

Walking and standing were once more kept at a minimum in the rest areas due to the ever-present enemy artillery shells and their dreaded shrapnel. Much of the time was spent sitting and crawling on the ground until they returned to the front line.

The Japanese were ingenious with respect to their artillery. Despite all the naval gunfire and artillery fire poured onto them by U.S. forces, they were able to contend in that area until near the end of the battle. Up in the northern end of the island were numerous artillery pieces mounted on little flatcars similar to railway handcars. These were mounted on narrow-gauge tracks, their artillery pieces fixed in place on those little cars and concealed in the many rock formations and caves with the tubular portions of the cannons pointing southward toward U.S. lines. When ready to fire, the enemy crews opened the doors at cave entrances, rolled cars with their artillery pieces out forward, fired a few rounds, and rolled the cars back into the security of the caves before counterfire was returned. The crews and the weapons were unharmed. Their guns were hard to spot from U.S. positions and even harder to hit.

On D+14 the advanced frontline Marine units reached the edge of the third and still-unfinished airstrip, and the rest period was now over as they prepared to return to the front. The following day what remained of the Second Battalion relieved elements of the Twenty-sixth Regiment and went back into the assault, with Easy Company on the left, Fox Company on the right, and Dog Company in reserve. This time the conflict was to be in the rocky, cave-infested region known as "No-Man's Land." It was spooky to see. Fellow Marines from the region of the North Dakota Badlands considered the area more similar to that bizarre area of their state than any other of their sites of battle.

From the military standpoint, the ground there was so broken, so rough, it was impossible for supporting weapons like half-tracks or 37mm guns to help. It was creep, crawl, blast, and burn for the infantry. The ground was hot. Insulation against the heat, if any, helped little, although it beat being cold at night. During the next two days the enemy opposition in that particular zone came from the elite of the Iwo Jap forces. These men were all large compared to most Japanese men. Many approached six feet in height. They were exceptionally well trained, expert marksmen who never surrendered. For them, like most Marines, it was a fight to the finish.

During the next two days the Marines made repeated but unsuccessful attacks against the Japanese lines. On March 6 alone eight men of Easy Company were killed and in Fox six; a total of eighty-one men in those companies were wounded. On March 7, Dog Company moved up to the front line. All three companies had fruitless experiences, making only a 200-yard advance to show for their combined efforts. All three units were running short of officers and NCOs.

On March 8, D+17, the Japanese resistance broke under a terrific drive led by Easy Company in what would usually be described as a banzai-like charge. The drive netted 300 yards, resulting in the death of 100 enemy troops. The charge, led by Lt. Jack Lummus, was a costly one. He was assigned to this company to provide leadership. Many plastic mines dotted the front before the Japanese line as well as behind it. Lieutenant Lummus stepped on one of those antipersonnel mines. It shattered his lower extremities as well as sadly mutilating him otherwise. Back at Camp Pendleton, he had been the commander of Menges's company. As an athlete of unusual prowess, Lummus had played in professional football ranks. Dog and Fox Companies, that day, measured their gains in relatively few yards. But the obstinate, formidable enemy line was breached.

That night the troops were told an all-out attack was scheduled for the next morning. Gen. "Howling Mad" Smith issued a written statement that circulated among the men. In essence it said: "You are holding up further operations, and we must wrap up this campaign quickly. Fleet units needed elsewhere are tied up, and we need to free them for other duties. Then, too, you are all that are left and you must carry it through to the finish." In effect he told them to stay up in the front lines until killed, wounded, or the enemy was finished. No more rest at the rear—no more relief—no more replacements. Until that moment most men had given their best and sacrificed in great quantities of personal destruction and life itself. His message was not a bit stirring. It did not go over well with the troops.

Later, Gerald Hemminger, a Blackfoot Indian from Minnesota, shared a foxhole with Menges. They compared notes and Gerald told him if he "bought it" in the next day or so he wanted Menges to have his blue-barrel, the special pistol he had, as well as the Japanese battle flag encased between his helmet and helmet liner. In return, Menges offered Hemminger the fifty dollars cash he carried in his breast pocket Bible, should he be the unlucky one. Hemminger was always broke. Menges later recalled, "I knew he could use the money. He was the sole support of his mother and two younger sisters back in the States. Consequently, he sent his service paychecks home to them. They lived on an Indian reservation and possessed little or nothing of worldly wealth. He never went on liberty or to a slop chute for beer, or even to a free movie. Except for a few toilet articles and personal effects, he lived a Spartan existence in order to help his mother and sisters."

They moved into position early in the morning before sunrise, and attack got under way about 0900 with, once more, Easy on the left and Fox on the right. Some advancement was made, but progress broke down because of the nightmare terrain and mounting casualties. The companies retired to original positions to regroup and prepare for another go at it.

The next attack began at 1400 in the afternoon. It, too, proved devastating. After a short gain, the attack broke again, and many casualties caught bullets right through the head. Included in this group was Menges's foxhole buddy, Hemminger. Menges really felt badly about Hemminger because he was a nice, caring guy who sacrificed for others. Today the loss of Hemminger still endures in Menges's mind.

Thereafter, the matter of caring for casualties confronted Fox Company. Though taking ground, they couldn't hold it, because one or two men were needed to evacuate each of the wounded. Numbers were dwindling. Effectiveness in the front line was reduced.

The company was reorganized. Again disaster struck. Platoon Sgt. Steve Hershberger came forward to the lines to reposition people before the jump-off—the beginning of the attack. Menges and Ed Simonsen, the old man of the platoon, were in the same foxhole. Sgt. Hershberger came through the rocks at the rear and stopped to chat for a few moments. Menges knew Hershberger as his mentor and friend from the early days of training, when Hershberger more or less took Billy under his wing and he really needed some guidance and direction. During a lull in action the day before the attack, Hershberger came to Menges's foxhole and they talked at some length as they had on several occasions previously. Hershberger told Billy, "You know, you could achieve much if you would change your attitude a little and become more cooperative." At that time, Hershberger was the best friend Billy had in the Marine Corps. As Hershberger stood there in the rocks behind them, he took a round right through the brow and fell dead on the spot. For Menges that was another grievous, terrible loss.

The next day was just as costly. The platoon guide, Albert Maeder, was hit by mortar fire and died after evacuation from the field. Platoon Sgt. Gibson, the hero at Death Valley, was hit in the leg by a sniper and had to leave. Another of Fox Company's valuable corpsmen was hit by mortar shrapnel in the hip and had to be evacuated. All but one of the original officers were gone. Of the original 234 Marines and 7 corpsmen, only 40 or 50 Marines remained. The cooks and bakers filled gaps in the line.

Early in the afternoon yet another attack was launched to try to finish the battle. Because all the NCOs were gone, Staff Sgt.

Ben Moffatt of the mortar section was brought up to help in the lines. Because he had been in the mortar section in the rear, Moffatt unwittingly proceeded to move out in front, walking upright. Within minutes he was killed. On Iwo one did not successfully lead attacks standing upright, and Moffatt paid dearly.

Word came to return to the starting point and hold whatever gains they could. En route back Menges jumped into an elongated trench line for a short respite and sat down, hands on knees, looking forward toward the enemy. His gaze wandered about and down to the sight of a third hand protruding upward between his legs. He came back in focus in a hurry, stood up, and took a hand count. He realized he inadvertently had sat on the back of a dead enemy soldier and thus had acquired a third hand! He and Ed Simonsen counted forty-two additional bodies of the enemy lying in that trench.

Menges's company made no progress that day. Both the platoon and company were shot up. The viability of 2-27 as an aggressive military force dwindled even further. It was a spent unit. For some unapparent reason Menges's right hand throbbed. He awakened the following morning with a greatly swollen red painful hand. He had taken a small piece of shrapnel in it on D-Day and it bugged him a little from time to time thereafter, but now it was streaked with red markings. He showed it to the remaining corpsman, Paul Bradford, who sent Menges right on back for medical attention. It looked like blood poisoning. The 2-27 Aid Station, swamped with casualties, referred him on back to the Fifth Division Hospital. That facility also overflowed with work and sent him as a walking casualty to the nearby Thirty-eighth Army Field Hospital, brought up from Saipan to help. There a young Army doctor set him on an empty orange crate to examine the hand. Without any sedatives or local anesthetic, he sliced open the thumb and squeezed out much pus. A gauze drain was inserted and a few days' supply of sulfa tablets handed to Menges. He bunked in for two nights and returned to his unit with a recommendation for light duty only—whatever that is during war. By then 2-27 enjoyed reserve status and the battle dwindled to a close.

When the brave fraction of the Twenty-seventh Regiment sailed away from the crucible of the last thirty-six days, few of those aboard turned back for a last look. Most preferred it fade into oblivion. The battered residuum of the Twenty-seventh Regiment gradually uncoiled from the constant tension that began when they poured out on the ocean's surface from those amphibious tractors aeons ago. The luxuries of good food, hot baths, shaved faces, and clean dungarees slowly diminished but never completely dissolved the hollowness of their cheeks and eyes. The happy-go-lucky joviality of youth long since left them, and the ringing voices no longer filled the air with their conversations. Teenage daredevil personalities gave way to maturity and softer, quieter voices in many, at least for the time being. Faraway stares and meditative periods of silence possessed many and became more frequent. Altered emotions and different values subconsciously replaced those of prebattle days. The hard scars of the loss of former buddies contracted within ever so unkindly, and a deep, deep persistent longing for home and loved ones endured above all else.

4

Death Valley—Soliloquies

Doubtless hundreds of battle sites have been tagged with the appellation *Death Valley* in the centuries of mankind's pursuit of the foolishness called war. Alfred Lord Tennyson, famous poet laureate of England, in 1855 wrote his dramatic poem, "The Charge of the Light Brigade." A few lines of it read: "Cannon to the right of them / Cannon to the left of them / Into the Valley of Death / Rode the six hundred." Three such areas were labeled Death Valley on Iwo Jima. One was in the Fourth Marine Division area in the eastern part of the island. A second was the region also known as the *Gorge,* near Kitano Point at the north end. The third Death Valley on Iwo lay between the northwest tip of Airfield #1 and the southwest corner of Airstrip #2. An exciting, devastating, brief skirmish transpired there. It extended to the crest of the west beach and was so named by the Marines who entered it on D+5 and who survived the fateful assault.

The night of D+4, Dog Company of 2-27 moved from its reserve position behind 2-26 to fill gaps in the line in event of a nocturnal banzai by the enemy. That tactic temporarily excluded Dog Company from the skirmish that occurred late the following afternoon. On the previous day the sight of the flag rippling in the bright sunlight and breeze above Mount Suribachi stirred all emotionally. We presumed the battle for Iwo was almost over; such was not the case. Since the log of our aid station is forever lost, its location on the day of the assault at Death Valley cannot be identified with finality, but our aid station was alongside an embankment of the first airfield and not very far south of the jump-off area.

Through the years, and in particular at reunions of the Fifth Marine Division Association, I heard and continue to hear repetitive mention of Death Valley. A mystic air of unrevealed importance was attached to that name in my mind. Until I read the memoirs of Col. Bill Menges, USMC (Ret.), an explicit understanding of that firefight was never my pleasure. The skirmish was a very intense, brief affair and was so destructive it imposed a deleterious effect on our battalion as a fighting unit. It was severely reduced in fighting power by the marked losses in troops it experienced there.

Much earlier on D+5, Easy and Fox Companies moved into adjacent positions for the jump-off and waited, Easy Company on the right flank, Fox Company on the left. Prior to the assault, Easy rotated a sharp ninety degrees left in order that Fox move through it to position itself on the right flank of Easy. Earlier in the day a lone tank had moved down through the valley and encountered no resistance until one of its tracks was shattered by a land mine. Its crew evacuated the lonely monster through its escape hatch on the bottom and walked unmolested to friendly troops far to the rear.

*   *   *

The order came at 1500 to move into Death Valley—Fox Company on the right flank, Easy on the left. Mike Ladich described it well when he noted:

> Death Valley? How could I ever forget it? We moved out in single file parallel to Easy when machine guns began to fire. I saw our men dropping. Some of them were hit. I went down on my stomach in that soft volcanic ash. Ed Perry lay immediately in front of me. We were fortunate to be positioned in that ash as we dropped to the ground. It sloped lower toward my position. I was down lower than

24

Ed, approximately three inches or more. The fire was intermittent and seemed to move horizontally, but not vertically. Bullets began to chip away at the base of Ed's spine. I was only a few feet away from him and could see what was happening. As the bullets hit him, bits of flesh and blood spattered on me. A hollow sound began to develop, and I could actually see the bared end of his spine emerge. The bullets did not penetrate his sides or hips. Like flat rocks thrown to the surface of water, they were skipping off the middle of his lower back.

Some of those same bullets hit my pack and tore it to shreds. I could hear the mess gear in it clatter when struck. The pack was torn to shreds, and I felt the impact of the bullets against my pack. Since I was lying on ash, I began to move it from under my abdomen with my hands, thereby lowering myself deeper into the ground. I noticed a small hole back about six feet and to the right. I edged backward and my foot dropped into the hole. I kept moving backward until I was entirely in it. I put my BAR down, took off my pack, and crawled back to Ed. I grasped his right foot and dragged him back into the hole. I poured sulfa crystals into his wound, stuffed as many bandages into it as I could, and called for a corpsman.

Lt. Tilghman, our platoon leader, was lying a short distance ahead behind a dirt embankment which partially encircled a pillbox. I crawled over near him. On the opposite side of Lt. Tilghman was the body of Robert Goff. A bullet smashed through his head and tore away the back part of his skull. His brains poured out on the ground.

Looking down at Goff, then at us, Tilghman instructed, "Keep your heads down. I'd rather meet you on Liberty in L.A. than bury you here." I've always respected him for that remark, and for his sensitivity to the horror around us. Tilghman called for a tank to help us. My foxhole buddy Louis Heminger and I were behind a large boulder when the tank came rumbling up to us. The hatch opened and a head emerged. He asked us the whereabouts of the pillbox causing all the trouble. We had spotted it a few minutes earlier. We pointed to the opening about six inches wide and eighteen inches high. A burst of machine gun fire ricocheted off the tank. The tanker ducked down inside. The tank's machine guns returned fire into the opening of the pillbox. They silenced the machine gun inside. We could see their bullets pouring in through the aperture. As the tank moved forward toward the pillbox, its 75mm cannon lowered and fired three or four rounds directly into it. When the shells exploded inside, the pillbox literally rose up from the ground and shuddered. Following the destruction of that installation, the tank crew stayed on to assist if needed.

As we walked away from the tank, Heminger and I stumbled upon Adolph Fang lying on the ground and bleeding profusely. Five machine gun bullets hit him in the chest. Menges and I draped him over our shoulders as we stood one on each side. We lifted him onto the tank deck, and placed him in a semi-sitting position leaning against the turret. In his inimitable way he joked, "Think I'll get the Purple Heart for this?"

He added, "Thanks. See ya, guys." What a show of courage. Here he was bleeding to death and still jocularly emitting his ironic humor. Until forty years later, I didn't know whether he lived or died.

*   *   *

Prior to the jump-off, Allan Mortenson, another rifleman in the same platoon, snapped a few pictures of the area with his Brownie Kodak camera. He noted:

I remember narrow boards with Japanese characters on them driven vertically into the ground. The position where they stood was the only logical spot to place machine guns where they could give us overhead, protective fire. It was also a great place for our small mortars serving the same purpose, providing overhead, protective fire. I believe those boards were artillery test-firing markers, pre-tested for their fire on us in event they spotted our troops occupying the positions. Earlier in the battle, I noted the enemy sometimes let us take positions they intended to defend, and did not fire at us until we moved to assault their interlaced, underground pillboxes. Earlier that day a tank ventured a long way ahead into the amphitheater unopposed until one track was blown away by the explosion of an underground land mine. The crewmen got out and returned to our lines unopposed.

Nothing was in front of us but open ground. It gradually led downward. About three o'clock we were ordered out of positions to move forward in a rapid charge. Almost immediately the enemy opened up with a variety of weapons, artillery, sniper fire, machine guns, mortars. Those in front did not catch the brunt of fire initially. Clarence Milburne was a machine gunner at the takeoff point. A sniper's bullet entered the front of his helmet. It traversed a path between the helmet and its liner to exit at the back. When later we were ordered to withdraw, I shared his foxhole and saw his helmet. He was shook up, but I don't remember his going back for medical attention. Maybe he did.

As the live fire began, I was on the right flank and sought protective cover in a large shell hole. George Piotrowski was already there and told me to look elsewhere, as he did not want enemy fire attracted to the site. I looked around, saw no other suitable cover, and stayed put. Ed Perry came along and got into the same shell hole. Piotrowski told him the same thing. Ed withdrew. Soon a flurry of machine gun bullets came toward us. George and I were in pretty good cover. I took two rounds of machine gun bullets, but not in my body. One round cut off the handle from my trenching shovel attached to my back pack. The other entered my pack, was slowed down by the contents and stopped at my clothing.

Ed Perry took the brunt of the machine gun fire, I saw Paul Bradford attending him. He gave him a shot of morphine, and dressed his wounds. Fortunately Billy Menges came up from the rear of our platoon, saw the emplacement and took it out.

The next thing I remember a huge buzz bomb lobbed toward our position. I hugged that shell hole to protect myself. That six feet or more of black powder and steel exploded and threw dirt, powder and steel all over the place. Either the people near the enemy pillboxes took them out, or the enemies within were as scared as everyone else by that unpredictable buzz bomb. A couple of fellows hauled Ed Perry out on a poncho and didn't stop until they reached the beach.

With so many of the platoon killed or wounded, we were ordered to withdraw to the starting point. Those of us who were lucky were now ordered to take up positions of defense. A unit of tanks came through our lines, and cleared the way to the cliffs ahead. After a scary night, a very thin line of Marines was pulled off the front the next morning.

Death Valley was shaped like an amphitheater. It was walled in by a sharp rise in the land to the east, which was an area between Airfields #1 and #2. The rise was joined with cliffs to the north. They extended almost to the sea. Behind those cliffs was Hill 362, the second most prominent place of Iwo Jima, and a natural for artillery emplacements of the enemy. Within minutes of our attack, forty men of Fox Company were killed or wounded. Dog Company was pulled into the skirmish and lost sixteen men just as quickly. Our advance was stopped cold. The first platoon was on the verge of being wiped out completely when Billy Menges stepped in and took a hand.

*　　*　　*

Keith Neilson, of Vancouver, Washington, submitted the following soliloquy. Keith was a Pfc. in Easy Company of 2/27, USMC, and in later years was a freelance writer.

Dear Dr. Brown,

I landed in the same amtrac as Captain McCann. My assignment on landing was to slash ropes holding ammo boxes on the fenders and push them off before the machine went back to sea. When I hit the sand, I was alone and started up the terraces of sand. I joined my two Raider Buddies and continued advancing. I saw a low-flying Corsair coming over us and, about 70 feet in front of us, I saw a double-barreled gun come up out of a hole and strafe the bottom of the plane. The plane made a half turn and crashed, just missing a amtrac of about the fourth wave. O'Bannon, Renshaw, and I got up and pitched hand grenades in on the gun emplacement. My first Jap was six feet away with a .45 caliber pistol in his face.

We went up and over and turned right and proceeded down a

gorge, but pulled back 100 yards to high ground. It was scary that first night expecting the banzai charges to come. They didn't. We had several rocket barrages from ships up close to our position. We had Jap shells coming in and one hit about 10 feet from us. I dived for the hole and I was hit by a piece of shrapnel in my left back. It hurt like thunder and my buddies patched me up. I decided that it was safer staying on the front line than trying to go back. You know what it was like back a ways. You were catching the full power of the Jap's big stuff. I spent two nights trying to retake the ground we had backed up from on the first night. I was supposed to be with Company so I went back to them. Major Salmon replaced Capt. McCann, who had only lasted for about a hour before the wound in his throat.

Company C.P. was holed up in a blown-up coastal gun emplacement. I felt safe there. A box about 1 foot square by 6 inches deep was found in the debris. Was it a boobie trap? Was it tied down? Maybe it was. Corporal Wayne Dust was assigned to dig it out. The rest of us moved to the front opening while the box was carefully prodded by a bayonet, which finally turned it over. It was painted white and on the top was a red cross. It was the Japs' first aid kit.

The next morning I was instructed to run a telephone wire up to Lt. Kellog. Dust asked me if I felt good enough. As I left I was told to look for a sniper who was throwing bullets at the opening of the gun emplacement. I was going along that side hill when a bullet hit in the sand about 25 feet from me. and I dived for a small shell crater. I peeked over the edge and another bullet hit 15 feet away. The next was 10, then 5 feet. The bullets were in a line running back out to some rocks in the surf. I had him spotted. He had me zeroed in. I got my gear ready to go and came out of that hole running like a Blue Racer. He missed. When I got up to the line, I connected the phone and told the C.P. where the sniper was. Later Lt. Kellogg and I were sitting about 4 inches apart and almost shoulder-to-shoulder in a crater when a bullet hit in between us. It was probably from Japs on high ground. Our big guns were right in front of us when we would move forward 50 feet. We even had a 16 incher skip up very close and then fail to explode. We had many casualties. I always said that it took us a week to retake the ground we gave up the first night.

At about the middle of the campaign, Corpsman Ray Hansen dragged a tall BAR man with a severe leg/hip wound into a shell crater. Floyd Jump came by and asked, "Doc, do you need help?" "Yes, dig this hole a lot longer." Jump had just started digging when a big shell came over and blasted above them. Jump asked, "Doc, are you OK?" "Yes." "Well, I'm not." He had been hit in the face by shrapnel. Hansen gave him the compress he was preparing to use on the BAR man. Jump walked out, holding the compress on his face. Hanson treated the other man and had him carried away.

The evening after Lummus was evacuated was the worst ever. Just at dusk two Japs sneaked in and crawled up the foxhole of Hansen and Murrah. One of them jumped in. Murrah got him with his pistol. The Jap landed on Hansen and he kept saying, "Shoot him again." I got the other one. The next morning Ray found an unexploded Jap grenade by his head. The Japs kept coming in all that night, and many of our wounded were crying for help. They were all killed just before daylight.

I was with Lt. Kellog. He was gone when daylight came. I was in the hold alone when Don Johnson, of Seattle, joined me. He wanted to share my ammo. In a moment big mortar shells started coming in. Don got hit in the back of his helmet with shrapnel. It rang his bell but did not otherwise wound him. We saw parts of bodies going up in the air. Don had left his buddies in a big hole, where one was cooking rations. Three dead and Al Pogowaga with one foot gone and the other shattered. Al was from Boise. Ray remembers treating Al. One of the dead was headless. When the shells were coming in, a piece of shrapnel fell in my hole. Stamped on it was 83 mm. It was from our big mortars. I called on my phone and got the mortars stopped.

About a dozen of our original 250 men walked out on the 24th day. Well, I'm done, almost. Seven or eight years ago Hansen came out here. I had written him a few times and invited him. In responding to my invitation, he wrote, "I remember you, Keith. You were the one who was always exposing himself to the Japs." That has a less valiant and different meaning in today's society.

*   *   *

Lelon Young of Easy Company was the assistant to BAR man Leonard Tharien. The morning of D+5 they were over near the top of the west beach and just north of the end of Airstrip #1. He and another Marine were sent to the rear for rations. On arriving at the truck hauling the rations, the other man recognized the driver as a friend from his hometown, and the two of them fell into an animated conversation. Lelon put his load on his back and prepared to leave. The other Marine told him to go on, that he would soon follow, wanting to talk to his long-lost friend a few minutes longer. After hurrying along as fast as he could over a distance of about one hundred feet, Lelon heard a loud explosion to his rear. Looking back, he could see the dust and dirt settling over the spot where the truck previously stood. Both friends from the same town were killed. It was a close call, but similar incidents happened to Lelon from the beginning of the battle. It was just another in a continuing series of close ones. He hurried on back with the half-supply of rations for the day.

As Young looked out over the terrain ahead just before moving into the assault that afternoon, he failed to see anything especially striking about it. Everything was fairly quiet. Easy Company took quite a mauling the day before and was shorthanded at the start. Shortly after they started forward, the enemy began firing at them from all directions. Men were dropping all around him. Easy Company reached its maximum advance not too far up when a huge shell hole, caused by an explosion of one of those sixteen-inchers, suddenly appeared in front of them. Every man still on his feet jumped in it, for it was the only protective shelter available in the face of all that fire. Only fifteen to twenty fighting men still remained in the company, and all took cover in the same hole. Another large shell on the same pinpoint target might have killed all of them. All at once Leonard Tharien rolled into the hole. He was unconscious. There wasn't a mark on him.

For years Young never knew what happened to Tharien. One day, when Young was well into his retirement, his curiosity overwhelmed him. He contacted a Veterans Administration office and inquired whether it had information about Tharien. After several weeks, a letter arrived conveying the address and telephone number of Leonard Tharien in Pontiac, Illinois. Lelon called and subsequently drove to see his old buddy. Leonard related that just after Easy Company started forward an artillery shell had exploded nearby. He vaguely remembered that a corpsman, in futile effort, tried to start a unit of plasma in one of his arms. Then Leonard blacked out. Several days later he awakened in a military hospital. Except for a headache, all was well. The concussion from the shell burst did it. Before long he was normal again.

*   *   *

Dick Tilghman, lieutenant and leader of the First Platoon of Fox Company, replied to my letter of inquiry as follows:

You asked me about the battle that took place in Death Valley, near the airfields. My memory of those events is not as detailed as other accounts I have read by many of my friends who were in the battle. I often wonder why I cannot remember the specific instances mentioned by many of the NCO's and enlisted men. I believe it due to the fact that I was running around from place to place and seldom had the opportunity to study a situation for a protracted period of time. Most of the enlisted men would be located in one area for a period of time, and had a chance to observe the immediate ebb and flow of battle. I do not believe my poor memory of specific instances has too much to do with age, as my memory is still fairly good.

I do remember the order to move down a small hill to the left front as we tried to take the immediate area occupied by Japanese infantry. There was no question that we did not have any idea as to how many Japanese were in that vicinity. It turned out there were a lot of them. We were pinned down after moving a few yards.

Prior to this time, we requested tank support. A tank appeared on the scene firing in the general direction of the enemy. Unfortunately, one of the rounds hit one of our men in our machine gun crew. He lost a foot and part of his leg. I went over to the rear of the tank and grabbed the communication telephone to direct their fire. As was usually the case, this telephone was not very effective. I remember becoming frustrated and kicking the tank just as one might kick a flat tire today. Of course the appearance of the tank drew Japanese mortar fire and made things more difficult.

Just how much time this all took, I do not remember. I do recall we withdrew and fell back to our previous position. Particular attention was paid to get the wounded back, as well as those killed in that action. I don't think it was a military defeat. The action came in the afternoon. It was always prudent to fall back to prepared positions rather than to try to dig new foxholes in a defensive manner late in the day. Such a procedure is particularly true when one is talking of a relatively short distance lost or gained.

*   *   *

Here is what I remember about that day [wrote Wallace Shaklee of Vancouver, Washington]. We were dug in for the night on a little ridge with this little valley out in front of us. We didn't know it at the time, but the Japs had pill boxes on the other side of that valley. The next day we charged out into the valley. They were laying for us, and they opened up on us with machine guns and mortars. Harley "Jack" Welch and I were foxhole buddies all through the operation. When all that firing started, Jack and I dove into a shell hole. Ed Perry hit the deck, maybe ten or fifteen yards from us. Ed couldn't get low enough, and a Jap machine gunner was raking Ed across the back. I guess it was Tilghman who saw the mess we were in and passed the word down the line to grab the wounded and fall back.

I got out my poncho and held one end. Jack held the other. We came out of that shell hole and scooped Ed up on a dead run. We got him back to where we were dug in the night before. We had so many casualties that day, there weren't enough stretcher bearers to care for them. I guess some of the walking wounded carried Ed back to the beach on my poncho.

Three or four days after that, something happened that I will never forget. Tommy was a nineteen-year-old kid from Texas. Tommy and I were crouched down side by side and a Jap sniper got Tommy right in the chest. Tommy fell over against me crying, "Momma, Momma, Momma" and that was it. I dragged Tommy over behind a rock and called for a corpsman. When Bradford got there, he said Tommy was dead.

*   *   *

Pfc. Austin Montgomery's perspective, as he recalled the fighting fifty-four years later, was somewhat different and also quite interesting:

I remember Death Valley quite well. I was the radio man for my platoon. Lt. Richard Tilghman was our platoon leader. I was feeling good after seeing Old Glory flying over Mt. Suribachi. At least we knew we would not catch any more fire from that direction. As we got our orders to push off, it was quiet before the storm. We moved a short distance when all hell broke loose. The Japanese soldiers probably had their orders to hold that strip of ground at all costs. We had ours to take it. They had fire trenches set up with machine guns knowing that we would hit those trenches for cover. There were little berms, also, behind which they could hide. Coots McGhee spotted a Japanese soldier behind a small berm, and he called to Hemminger (whom we called Little Chief) to stay down, that there was a Jap behind it. Little Chief raised his head to see the Jap and got a bullet between the eyes. He was the first one to be killed at Death Valley. They hit us with mortars and everything they had.

I had several requests over my radio for stretcher bearers. A little later in the day, Lt. Tilghman and I saw at least five of the enemy dive head first off the cliffs on the other side of the Valley, and down to their deaths on the rocks below as they committed suicide.

His comment was, "Wouldn't it be nice if the rest of them would do likewise."

As I remember, early the next morning we crossed over Death Valley. Then we were relieved for a short rest a few days. Then we took our position on the left of the line again. It was something I never want to go through again. But, I'm glad I had the experience of combat. Perhaps if I had been wounded, I would feel different.

I have always had a big spot in my heart for corpsmen. They took care of the wounded without regard for their own safety. In 1995 at an Iwo Jima reunion in Atlanta, Georgia, the program was a tribute to the corpsmen of Iwo Jima. It was a very moving program and I can tell you there was not a dry eye in the house.

It has been over fifty-four years since we went through that hell. Some things may have been forgotten so we can keep sane minds.

*   *   *

Pfc. Lou Balog was a flamethrower in an assault squad in Dog Company. As noted previously, Dog Company was moved from its reinforcing positions with the Twenty-sixth Marines to replace Fox Company of our battalion after Fox was so badly shot up and disorganized, it could no longer function as a company. The rest of the day Dog Company remained fixed in its new positions and foxholes. Following some air strikes and intense fire power by assisting tanks, Dog Company moved forward the next day, D+6, into and through Death Valley:

We advanced northward along the west side of the island until we were pinned down. I stood behind a scrubby tree. Another man came up closely behind me and leaned against me. I told him to keep close, but did not look back. When we got the order to advance again, I stood up and looked back at whoever was behind me. He fell over as I stood. His head was hanging by a few strings of flesh: it was cut off by shrapnel, probably, and all that time his body was leaning against me.

It was raining that morning and I was soaking wet. As we advanced, I looked about. Over to one side was the body of dead Marine lying under ponchos. I hate to say this, Dr. Brown, but I undressed the dead comrade except for his dungaree blouse with his name on it, and swapped my wet clothes for his dry ones. I asked the Good Lord to forgive me.

Our platoon leader was Lt. James Ronan. He and Bill Autry and myself were pinned down in a foxhole. The Lieutenant was studying to be a priest when he volunteered for the Marine Corps. I asked him what his plans were for after the war, and whether he still planned to enter the priesthood. He said, "Lou, I am going to die right here in the Marine Corps." A few minutes later he stuck his head up to look around, and a sniper got him right between his eyes. He fell back into my left arm. The back of his head was completely gone. I found it hard to forget.

Several days later we were preparing for another jump-off. Joe Czerniawski and I grew up together in Cleveland, Ohio, where we joined the Marine Corps together. That morning he asked me to let him go get water for the platoon. He insisted and took off down a draw. The Japs started shelling. I saw Joe fly up in the air when a shell landed near him. The next time I met Joe was back in Cleveland. He was completely emasculated by shrapnel from that shell and was injured in one leg so it was shorter than the other. Later he went to California, where he committed suicide. I often wonder why I didn't go for the water that day.

Later that day when we were pinned down, I was asked to hit a cave with my flame thrower. I was standing on a bluff about fifty feet above it. We were taught to spray the fuel into such caves, then to ignite it. The force of the explosion blew the flame thrower and myself what seemed like seventy feet into the air. The weapon was shooting flames all the way down. Men of a Howitzer crew came over when I landed. The left side of my face and body was flaming. They extinguished the fire, but had to go back to our Aid Station for treatment of their burned hands. Someone covered my eyes. As I lay on a stretcher, other wounded and I heard yelling and shots. Being unable to see, my imagination ran wild about what was happening. When it was all over a corpsman gave us something to quiet us, and told us some Japs infiltrated the defense to kill their own wounded. People to whom I told this story later seemed to doubt it. We knew the truth.

*　　*　　*

The following are Bill Bainter's recollections of that skirmish. Bill was a BAR man in Fox Company:

Dear Doc,

This is what I recall about Death Valley. As we came into the low area, a small explosion erupted between Andy Dupal and me. Neither were hurt. At this time a Jap machine gun opened up adding more incoming rounds to the already plentiful supply. About ten to fifteen yards in front was a slightly elevated bit of ground with a bush at its highest point. I headed for it. Someone yelled, "Pillbox in front." As I looked from behind the bush, I could see the pillbox and through the slit-like firing opening, I could see a shadow moving within. At this time I fired a few rounds for effect. Suddenly, George Goff, an assault squad Bazooka man, appeared to my right. Not seeing anyone with him, I asked if he needed help loading. He said he did not need help since the weapon was loaded and ready to fire. I then fired a few more rounds into the pillbox even though there was no apparent movement within at the time. I told Goff I would give him covering fire while he took aim. Not hearing an answer, I looked at him and he had removed his helmet. I yelled at him to put it on. He replied he could not see very well to aim when he wore the helmet. At that second a crease appeared across his skull and grew ever wider and wider.

I yelled so others could hear that a sniper was watching from near the pillbox. Then an explosion occurred in the pillbox. Whether it was Menges' grenade or something else, I do not recall.

Later I heard Sergeant Gibson's voice calling to us to get the wounded off the field. Later, and after talking to others, I came to the conclusion that Sergeant Gibson deserved far more recognition than the Bronze Star Medal. A Silver Star Medal would have been minimal recognition for what he accomplished.

37

*   *   *

Pfc. Jay Rebstock manned a BAR in an assault squad in the Second Platoon of Easy Company. He wrote:

Dear Doc,

Our Company Commander, Captain Billy McCann, was shot in the neck as he moved across the beach just after landing. Lieutenant Frank Fitch, his executive officer, took over command of the company. A few days later he was wounded by a piece of shrapnel which cut a hole in his chest. Lt. Fred Kellogg was our platoon leader. Platoon Sergeant James Comstock was killed on D-Day.

Iwo Jima was a small island. It was filled with enemy troops from one end to the other, and from side to side when we landed. For those reasons a flank attack was impossible. Every morning about eight o'clock, our artillery and mortars fired overhead at Jap front line positions. For the first four or five days in the early part of the battle, at the designated time, they were joined by big artillery of offshore battle ships. They sailed away a few days after D-Day. When the designated moment came for us to attack head on, those weapons lifted their over head fire. Immediately the Japs would come out of their holes and caves and other positions and clobber us.

Someone decided to change the strategy on D+5. We did not move into jump-off positions until early afternoon and there was no pre-attack bombardment. With all this change, we were hoping to surprise the enemy. Major Jack Salmon took over command of our company. We began our advance moving parallel to the low-lying cliffs bordering the western beaches. There were lots of small bushes in front of us. The terrain over which we moved was very uneven. This not only made moving over it somewhat difficult, but it also rendered vision spotty ahead of us.

As we moved forward, the ground gradually sloped downward. When we came to that level piece of ground we named Death Valley, the Japs opened up on us with everything they had, airburst shells, mortars, artillery, machine guns and rifle fire. It

38

was so thick we couldn't tell where it all came from. Finally someone ordered up a couple of tanks. They fired over our heads at targets just forward from us. That gave us a chance to jump out and run for a huge bomb crater in front of us for shelter. Corporal Herbert Green was shot in the front of his helmet. The bullet traveled around between the steel helmet and its liner and came out the rear. All he got out of it was a terrible headache and temporary loss of hearing.

The next thing I remember, another BAR man in our squad, Leonard Tharien, was hit by a mortar shell and I took over his weapon. All of a sudden there was a very loud explosion in the Jap lines. I found out later Leonard Nederveld threw a grenade in a Jap pill box. It set off one huge explosion which blew him and several of the enemy in the pill box up in the air. At the time one of our tanks was hit and also blew up with a tremendous force. Everyone stopped shooting, everyone, the Japs as well as us.

We were told to remove our dead and wounded and to retreat on back to the original positions of that morning. It rained all the next day. We stayed in our foxholes. Late in the afternoon we spotted someone crawling toward us from a considerable distance out forward. We thought it was one of the enemy. We noticed he would crawl a short distance, raise an arm, crawl a bit more and raise his arm again. We didn't realize he was trying to wave to us. We decided to let him crawl closer. Shortly after that, someone yelled, "It's a Marine." Two men ran out and carried him back to my foxhole.

A corpsman came over and checked him out. I had no idea who the man might be. Lt. Kellogg came to my hole, and told Louis Komenich and myself to get the man back to the Aid Station. We were ordered to go on back from there and get supplies. Two other Marines joined us to help carry the stretcher bearing the wounded man.

We were underway not more than a few minutes, when the Jap mortars started shelling all around us. We moved along as fast as we could and luckily found a large shell crater and jumped in it. I was calling the man by what I thought was his name, when Lou told me it was Nederveld, not Watson. His eyes were swollen and sticking out of their sockets. His face was chopped up and swollen. The skin of his arms and body was peppered with little pieces of steel. I just knew he was going to die.

In June 1947, I was in a class in a Business College, when who should walk in but Leonard Nederveld. I was so startled I could have dropped over. He is still receiving 100% disability for his wounds. (Forget all the mistakes in this, the longest letter I have written in seventy-five years.)

*   *   *

Like his friend, Jay Rebstock, Leonard Nederveld was a rifleman in Easy Company in the battle at Iwo. At the 50-Year reunion of the Fifth Marine Division in St. Louis in 1995, Jay told me Leonard was in a fantastic incident in the skirmish at Death Valley. He mentions it in his contribution to this chapter. After locating Nederveld at the reunion, I requested an interview for the purpose of his version of that incident. His story was essentially as follows:

I spotted a bunker from which a machine gun was firing on some of our outfit. As I raised my M-1 to fire into the front side firing aperture, my squad sergeant told me to hold up. Instead of that he instructed, "crawl in a semi-circular path to the side of the opening and toss a grenade at it. It will stun everyone in there. Then toss in a second one to wipe them out." I crawled as ordered and tossed number one. It exploded and I pulled the pin on the second and tossed it right through the opening. I don't really know what happened after I tossed it in there.

Other squad members reported a tremendous explosion which blew the bunker apart. Bullets, rockets, shells, everything was flying every which direction all over the area. One Marine was injured by a wild missile. In another minute or two a second and similar explosion occurred with the same results. Everyone hit the deck and stayed there until it was all over. Then there was absolute quiet on the part of both the enemy and the Marines. Nederveld was not to be found anywhere. He was presumed killed by the first great blast.

He continued his story and said to me:

It seemed to be the morning of the next day when I was awakened by bright sunlight shining in my eyes. I felt horrible due to a terrific headache. I could see the cliffs forward from me, the same ones I saw ahead of us when we started down into the valley. I realized I was in front of our position. I did not move for a long time for fear the enemy would spot me and shoot me.

Nothing happened. It must have been about two o'clock in the afternoon when I decided to go for it. I rolled over on my front side. I reached forward with my right arm, because my left arm was weak. I crooked the right arm at the elbow and pulled with it. At the same time I shoved a bit with my feet. I did not have much power, but this effort enabled me to move forward a little bit. No one fired at me. The process was slow, but little by little I was getting closer. My vision was blurry, but finally I made out the forms of two Marines appeared through my dim vision. I looked up and saw one sighting in on me with his rifle. I yelled, 'Don't shoot. Don't shoot.' My voice was so weak he may not have heard me.

Suddenly the other man with him shouted, "Don't shoot. He's a Marine." The two of them came forward and drug me back into their lines. Some of the fellows put me on a litter and started carrying me on further back. All at once an artillery bombardment started, and they shoved me down the side of a big hole. I was so weak I passed out. When I came to, I was on another island somewhere, and in a military hospital. Several months later I was released from a hospital back in The States and returned home. A lot of shrapnel remains in my body from whatever happened after that second grenade.

Several years later I was told that bunker was a large one used for munitions storage. It was connected by a tunnel to another bunker just like it. I must have had a concussion from the blast and missed out on all the fireworks.

41

*   *   *

Chuck Allman was a rifleman in the Third Platoon of Fox Company on D+5.

Our platoon was in reserve. So many men were already lost by that time, our lines were stretched a bit thin. Our platoon was moved up and over on the right flank of Fox Company to fill a gap between it and a unit of another regiment still further to the right . We moved forward with everyone else. Suddenly the Japs opened up from everywhere with their machine guns. Then they began bombarding our area with mortars and artillery. I jumped into a shell hole with four or five other Marines. Judson Bay, our squad leader, yelled, "Some of you guys get out of here. There are too many of you bunched up in here. You will draw a lot of fire and we'll all be killed."

I started up out of the hole. Just as I went over the edge, a big mortar shell, like a ninety mm, streaked over me. It exploded in the hole, but I didn't hear any explosion. A rush of warm air seemed to push me up and forward. I came down running. I hurried on forward a short distance and hit the deck. George Nelson was fatally injured. All the rest were wounded, including Judson Bay, who told us to get out of the hole. There was no sound, just a hot wind that threw me through the air. I came down with my legs still pumping and I didn't stumble. I stayed on my feet still running. Others, including the one who told us to get out, were wounded. I forgot to thank him. Ralph Baker died of gunshot wounds later as we came up the first hill beyond the valley. It wasn't long until we were ordered to pull back to the starting area. Someone told us to take the dead and wounded who could not walk on back along with us. I remember litter bearers carrying out the First and Second Platoon wounded until quite late that night.That was a close call.I made it through the rest of the battle o.k.

*   *   *

On reading Corpsman Roy Brown's response, I felt it was evident that he did experience some significant changes due to an almost tragic encounter with a near-miss artillery shell. He wrote:

Physicallly I am devoid of any problems relative to my combat experience. My psychological problems began Aug. 12, 1944, the day we left Camp Pendleton for Hawaii. On that morning I called my parents in Los Angeles. Mother was home and I wanted to bid her, "So Long."

Mother never said goodbye. However, as she hung up she said, "Goodbye, Bud. If any thing happens to you, I shall kill myself." As I was her only child, I knew she meant it. Still have a problem with that artillery round that hit in front of me and exploded under me. I still see the steel glint of that round just before it hit. Perhaps I dwell on that because I realize that one round robbed me of my ability to function anywhere near maximum efficiency.

I seem to recall an article in *Leatherneck,* 1945, "The Twenty-seventh Marines Banzai Charge." But the best I could come up with was the article Rondero sent titled, "They Called It Death Valley." My recollection of it is that [person's name withheld], who landed with Easy Company, wanted to be relieved. He came to the Aid Station wild-eyed. Dr. Collins told us since I trained with Easy Company, I should take his place, and also that Easy Company was in reserve. I gathered all my gear and took as much of rations as I could carry, and worked my way up to Easy. I checked in with the first platoon and proceeded to have "lunch." The guys kept staring at me and I asked when they were going to eat. A sergeant said, "Doc, the only food we have had is what you brought up when you came for wounded." I distributed the rations I had brought along, and started to move around. I knew very few men in the first platoon. My time before had been with the third platoon and the mortar section.

Someone said, "Doc, you better stay down."

It was then I learned we were on the line and not in reserve. About that time I was clued in on what was to transpire. Easy Company was high up on a hill overlooking the valley. As I understood, Easy Company was to move forward in a quarter turn that would put them at the base of 362A depression. I'm sure Fox Company was on our left and the Twenty-first Marines on our right. Elements of the Twenty-first Marines (Third Division) were to move forward with us. Their objective was to go forward and over Hill 362A, albeit well beyond our range. The last thing I remember was jumping into a shell hole and catching that glint of the artillery round just before it hit right in front of me. I awakened half buried and blind. When I urinated blood, I flipped. I remember Joe Gordon pouring brandy in me. He said I caused him problems during the night. Later I learned the Twenty-first Marines never moved. Several years later, at a February Banquet at Camp Pendleton, they said they were pinned down by heavy mortar fire. I just smiled. They got the message.

*　　*　　*

Now a few comments from me, Joan [Brown], since you did ask me for comments and I never sent you any. Unlike many we have talked to, who apparently have deliberately erased memories of the horror of Iwo from their minds, Roy has retained many. He always had an exceptional memory, which I generally envy. I wonder whether he might have been better off to forget most of the Iwo campaign. We all deal with life in unique ways. His has been to "re-hash" and undoubtedly that is a part of his excellent memory. It has also affected the tranquillity of his life. He used to have dreadful, different dreams. On one occasion he had the window screen out, and was poised to jump when I awoke and woke him. There is no question he suffered "survivor's remorse."

Death of a Marine

In this bomb-scarred battlefield we waked with sunlight's first
    beams.
A cynic spark within your soul begat a song, "Oh, what a
    beautiful morning."
The high-pitched hiss of snipers' speeding bullets replied in
    monotone.
Back into our foxholes we dove.

Hours later we knelt on either side,
There by our comrade whose mangled thigh
Was severed by a shaggy piece of shrapnel.
You stanched the flow of blood by pressure
Just above the tattered end of a fluent artery.
After morphine, I started plasma.
A mortar shell exploded to our left.
We both looked, and back I glanced to you.
A hideous sight! There in a moment,
In the twinkling of an eye, you exploded
There before me as did that first shell.
My sight was gone. It had to be the end.
Blood coursed my cheek, my brow,
And on down into my mouth.
Reflexly then with senseless hand I wiped my eyes.
Behold! The plasma dripping in the vein as drip it should.

A shard of pointed, hard, warm bone
Had pierced my blouse. And on my belt
A piece of flesh slowly oozed its last.
Across my outstretched arms your entrails lashed.
And mushy excrement marked: FINIS.
Your salted blood oozed within my lips
Into my gaping mouth,

An evil eucharistic rite to Mars. You! My own brother!
Sacrificed upon the cross of this unholy war.
A direct hit.
The comrade with the shattered limb
And I were left to grieve.

O Mother dear, your letter asking
How he died befell my lot.
Our colonel handed it to me and choked—
"Here, Hal, this one is yours. You saw it all."
And, so, my answer. Forever seemed its coming.
You'll sense it so acutely more than I,
That flash of darkness, that piece of bone,
The innermost; your very own,
That flow of blood.
The twinkling of an eye,
And nothing, nothing more was ever found.

Part II

The Wounds

5

Our Corpsmen

The U.S. Marine Corps is the amphibious arm, an integral part of the U.S. Navy. During World War II the medical services of the USMC were provided by the USN Medical Corps. Those enlisted men of the Navy who were assigned to basic medical training in U.S. Naval hospitals were designated with the rate Hospital Apprentice. From that rate such men moved rather quickly to the next higher, Pharmacist's Mate Third Class (or Ph M 3/C). The ladder of time, experience, and progress took them on up to Ph M 2/C, Ph M 1/C, and Chief Ph M in the Marine Corps as it would in the Navy. To assault infantry battalions were also assigned two medical officers who were medical doctors. The senior such medical officer held the rank of lieutenant in the Navy, the equivalent in rank to that of captain in the Army. The junior medical officer held the rank lieutenant, junior grade.

A half-dozen corpsmen entered Hq. Co. 2-27 the same day as I. The recently commissioned Fifth Marine Division was rapidly expanding personnelwise, and in another month it attained its full complement of officers and enlisted men. More corpsmen poured in almost each day. One of these was Chief Ph M Milt Klinger. In essence, he was the foreman, the leader, of the ultimate body of thirty-nine corpsmen plus himself. Being the only medical officer in the organization, I was the director. In two weeks I was superseded by a doctor with the rank of Lieutenant, M.C., USN. In a month or two, he was replaced by Lt. Tom Collins, M.C., USNR, who was also my superior medical officer.

At Camp Tarawa on the island of Hawaii, small Quonset huts were constructed in each battalion area to be the medical facility for each assault battalion. Each contained a field desk for record keeping and four to six folding canvas cots to serve as beds for in-patient Marines, ill with bad colds, influenza, serious gastrointestinal upsets, or infected wounds of one type or another. The in-patients were attended by Dr. Collins and myself, plus those corpsmen assigned to duty in our Sick Bay.

Here all members administered mass inoculations for typhoid, tetanus, and yellow fever. At a designated hour the troops began filing through the Sick Bay in a double line, passing by corpsmen who injected these vaccines in each man. Some company corpsmen requested the privilege of injecting the men of their own platoon. We honored those requests, since they provided valuable experience for the corpsmen. The permanent health records were kept and maintained in the Sick Bay. Entries were made in them of inoculations, injuries, transfers to hospitals, etc.

As time advanced and the battalion became more sophisticated in its training and maneuvers, Dr. Collins ordered me to instruct our corpsmen in the care of the wounded. Having never been in battle, I was truly a neophyte in that area. Some principles of first aid, as learned in Boy Scout days, provided a good beginning on the subject. Along the medical education route in medical school and internship, certain skills were learned that were basic for this work. A quantum of common sense helped. The corpsmen as well as I were undaunted by our ignorance, and we set about improving our skills for treating casualties.

Two corpsmen were assigned to our battalion's 90mm mortar platoon and one to the communications section. Each of these units was a part of Headquarters Company. Each rifle company, i.e., Dog, Easy, and Fox, contained three rifle platoons and a 60mm mortar platoon. Two corpsmen were assigned to each of these platoons, and a Ph M 1/C was designated to be head corpsman for the company medics. He was responsible for maintaining supplies, for liaison between those companies' headquarters and our aid station in the event of necessity, and for assisting the platoon corpsmen when needed. The remaining corpsmen worked in the Sick Bay in camp. When we went to Iwo, we left Bill Jeffreys behind to maintain and service the Personal Health Records of those missing in action, killed in action, or wounded and removed from action.

To train for management of the troops wounded in combat, groups of corpsmen and I met in the field behind our battalion area for instruction in differentiating between arterial and venous bleeding, stopping hemorrhages, injecting morphine from syrettes, splinting fractures, closing wounds with sutures or with adhesive tape, cleaning wounds, managing phosphorous burns, using small and large battle dressings, marking information on the red tags for the personnel at the next level of care, applying tourniquets, reconstituting blood plasma from dry powder and administering the aqueous solution intravenously, and using rifles, sticks, or whatever might be available otherwise for holding the intravenous plasma solution elevated during its administration. The corpsmen were intensely interested in learning.

The following is excerpted from a letter written to my wife from Camp Tarawa. It is included at this point since it reflects a momentary evaluation of some of our corpsmen five months before we engaged in battle.

Dearest Adeline,

This afternoon I called some of the more enterprising corpsmen together in the hope of obtaining their opinions as to wherein they felt they had insufficient training and what they desired to learn in the future regarding their duties in battle. It was astounding to listen to their excellent suggestions. During the past three weeks, we have had several sessions together, and yesterday's session included a field problem. Those fellows are quite eager to learn more and to become better corpsmen. Their sense of duty is sincerely profound. A pride exists in their work and in being corpsmen. As I said, they are aggressive young men, and probably surpass others in their individual abilities. Most of them are a year to nine years younger than yourself. A few are older. I fail to give them credit for being men who are just as I was a few years ago, and who would be doing things similar to what I did a few years ago if it were not for the war.

In due time, when we went into the field for company and battalion-strength maneuvers, some Marines, both men and officers, were tagged as casualties, and on the tags were names of simulated injuries. The corpsman did his thing in disposition of these feigned casualties, based on his training. I educated them as best I could, anticipating that should I be severely wounded, I would get appropriate care on the spot by some corpsman. This bit of training proved fruitful in combat. In the din, smoke, and dust of battle, those platoon corpsmen ran about from one wounded man to another applying proper treatment, all the while without concern for themselves. One item I did not anticipate was their care for the obviously dying. For this they called upon their own natural resources in instinctive manner. holding the dying in their arms those last few moments, comforting and listening.

In the months of training, some of the "Old Marines," those who had enlisted prior to Pearl Harbor, regarded some of our corpsmen with scorn and derision because they were "Navy," not Marines. The corpsmen resented such treatment but held their tongues. They lived with the men of their platoons and companies, often becoming fast friends, sometimes acting the part of the neighborhood parson or friendly psychiatrist. Often they shared good and bad news from home and enjoyed just being one of the gang. Their selflessness, courage, and commitment under fire were exemplary. Those Old Marines who survived became their greatest admirers. Three of these came to me at Sick Bay to apologize for their precombat derogatory remarks about corpsmen. Six of the original corpsmen were killed and twice as many wounded. Six received Navy Cross citations and three the Bronze Star Medal. Except for two, they all deserved such recognition. The wonderful behavior, their remarkable deeds under fire, were not due to any preaching or teaching by Dr. Collins or myself. Their devotion and sacrifice for their fellowmen came from within.

6
Hitting the Beach

As Told by Corpsman Roy Brown:

After we left the line of departure, the coxswain and I were chatting all the way to the beach. He was Regular Navy. So was I. As we cruised along in his LVT, he told me that at the battle for Tarawa his craft got hung up on a reef going in. That embarrassed him. He was determined to go all the way this time. He promised, "I'll get you there onto that beach. I'll take the governor off and rev it up to three thousand rpm. We'll get there this time."

We got in all right. Parked up front on the deck of the craft was a jeep loaded to the gills with mortar shells. After all the troops ran out over the lowered front ramp, he started to back off. That loaded jeep was so heavy it held the front end right down there in the sand and he couldn't pull it back into the ocean. He was really grinding away in the thick of the enemy fire. In a couple minutes I looked back and saw him finally pull away. While I was looking back at the LVT, out of the corner of my eye I saw a Marine floating in the water at the edge of the beach. I went back and pulled him farther up onto the sand. He was one of the Navajo Indians in our platoon. He started to sing some sort of Indian chant. I could see a bullet wound in his head. I took a syrette of morphine from my medical kit and gave it to him in the shoulder. Just then he went limp and died. He never really hit the beach.

I started forward once again and went up to the first level above the beach. I saw Elmo Eastman walking diagonally up the slope. Someone yelled, "Corpsman!" Elmo turned and waved me off as if to say that he could take care of the situation. He ran two or three steps forward and pitched over in the sand. I got there a few seconds later. He was dead, killed by a bullet through the head.

As I turned away to move on, I saw a fellow named Boyd of our platoon lying nearby on the ground. A piece of shrapnel had taken off a large piece of his skull. There was a lot of brain tissue hanging out. It sure was an ugly sight. I didn't know what to do, so I prayed, *O Jesus, help me, please.*

Just then Dr. Brown passed by and said, "Hold on there, Roy. I've never seen anything like that before, either. Just a minute and I'll help you." We covered his head with a large battle dressing. As we were doing that, Boyd jerked a couple of times, breathed very noisily, and relaxed. He was dead. We moved on up after that. Already in just a few minutes of landing I had witnessed three deaths.

I went up over the top right away. There I saw Seymour Sataloff, a corpsman in our company. He was just standing there holding his left arm. He said he was just hit by a piece of shrapnel flying through the air. When he reached over with his right hand to check it, he could feel the bare bone. I sprinkled the wound with a packet of sulfa crystals and put a battle dressing over it. I told Sataloff to go back down to the beach and await transportation back to a ship. Several months later back in the States, he told me that he waited there in all that clamor on the beach for four hours until he got a ride. After the wound healed, he had normal use of his arm.

By the time Sataloff headed back for the beach, Corpsman Graf was killed on the beach. Corpsman George was killed immediately after he went over the top. Elmo was already gone, leaving the care of the entire Easy Company to Wyeth, Murrah, Hansen, Moreno, Wallace, and myself.

A few days later up there by Hill #362 I was taking care of a lot of wounded. They were lying all around me. As I was moving about taking care of them one at a time, an artillery shell exploded right in front of me and blew me way up the air thirty feet, or so it seemed. After I hit the ground, I felt numb all over. For some crazy reason I thought that I was dead. After a while everything seemed to clear except a horrible, shaky feeling that seemed to be all through me. Finally, I was able to get up and start taking care of the wounded again. I went through the rest of the battle, miraculously, without another injury.

As Told by Corpsman Edward Jones:

Edward Jones enlisted in the U.S. Navy shortly after graduating from high school in Spokane, Washington. He had several classes in business education while in high school. At the time of the early organization of the Second Battalion, Twenty-seventh Marines, he was the only corpsman in our outfit who could type proficiently for our purposes. As a consequence, he became the clerk of our Sick Bay and assumed responsibility for all official entries required by the USN to be inscribed in the Personal Health Record of every individual in our battalion dating from the time of the man's entry into our outfit, throughout his stay in it, and until his exit.

In addition to the recording duties, Jones was one of the small group of corpsmen who assisted the battalion surgeons in caring for patients in occupancy of any one of the six infirmary cot spaces in our Quonset Hut Sick Bay erected in our battalion area. He also trained in the field occasionally with rifle companies. Moreover, he trained in our instruction courses in the field in the management of battle wounds. In battle he assisted in care of the wounded. He oversaw our medical supplies. He maintained the log of aid station admissions. He was obliged to keep all these duties in order as we moved along in combat every day or two in keeping with the forward movement of the battalion command post. Many years later he submitted the following account of those intense, exciting earlier hours of the assault on Iwo Jima as he observed them.

I still remember when we first landed on the beach and the front end of our LVT was tilted upward by some solid obstacle beneath the foresection. We all fell backward to the after end of the vehicle. We had to crawl all over and around one another to get out, dragging our baggage with us. They didn't train us in that method of evacuating the LVT, as I recall. I still had the duffel bag filled with fifty two-ounce vials of medicinal brandy. Back aboard ship the day before, Dr. Collins handed me that duffel bag along with the caveat, "Do not lose under any circumstances."

After crawling out of the LVT, I hustled forward as best I could through that black sand. About twenty yards inland, machine-gun fire from bunkers and other hidden places greeted us, spurting up sand as close as five feet from us. I hit the deck and heard someone with an authoritative voice yell, "MOVE OUT!" That helped me get going again. There were lots of others beside myself on the beach. Then a mortar shell exploded near me, leaving me deaf from the concussion. The hearing loss lasted for a half hour, then cleared completely.

Moving over the top of the beach and farther inland, I came upon my first casualty. He was a Marine who was hit in the right eye socket. His eyeball was hanging down from it. I did my best to push it back in place and applied a large battle dressing over it. Following a shot of morphine, I marked a large, red *M* on his forehead with merthiolate and told him, "Get back down there on the beach away from here and stay there. Someone will see that you get back to a ship." I never learned whether he made it. That beach was in such pandemonium. It was a horrible place to be.

My next casualty was a Marine who was hit in the buttocks by shrapnel. It was a bloody mess with half of one buttock just hanging there. I tried to put the piece back in place and applied a large battle dressing. I injected a shot of morphine in one arm and marked a large *M* on his brow with merthiolate. I told him the same thing; that was to get back to the beach and away from all this.

On arriving halfway across the island, I jumped into a large shell hole occupied solely by another Marine. His name was Jacobson. He was from my hometown, Spokane. I did not know him before that moment. He was an interpreter of the Japanese language. Being in charge of the duffel bag of brandy, I had one of those vials. It smoothed out everything for me. It calmed anxiety and restored reason. I offered him the other half. He was much worse off than I and had awful shakes due to fear. He must have deemed it poison or something bad. I could not persuade him to take so much as a sip. During the battle I kept a log of every casualty coming into the aid station for treatment. In addition I also logged the names of those in our battalion killed in action and those known to be treated elsewhere than in our facility. That duty was hard to take since I knew most of those fellows. After we returned to Camp Tarawa, I turned the log in at our battalion office. It was supposed to be sent someplace as a permanent record.

A particular event in our aid station left a lasting impression. It was the time Lieutenant Lummus was brought in on a stretcher. His legs were like toothpicks. His feet were gone. Spikes of bone were all that remained. There was little any of us could do in those primitive circumstances other than start plasma and keep him sedated until he was evacuated on back. I recorded him in our ledger.

I shall be ever grateful that I never had to relive those scenes over and over in my mind as others have through the years. I can recall some of them in an objective manner, Maybe I would have been more sensitive had I been older. Fortunately, I was but twenty years old and very naive.

As Told by Corpsman Jerry Cunningham:

I remember very clearly February 19, 1945, and the invasion of Iwo Jima. At 0300 we were roused from our bunks as clanging gongs and blaring loudspeakers screamed, "REVEILLE, REVEILLE!!" Before long we were up and dressed and on our way to breakfast. Scuttlebutt was that we would get real eggs and steak, a traditional last meal before hitting the beaches. I should have known better. Our chow line went right by the Officers' Mess. Sure enough, they were having the traditional—maybe there was real hope! As our line moved up ahead we could see what they were getting at the front end, scrambled powdered eggs and Spam! What a way to go.

After putting on all of my personal gear, I was standing beside Sgt. Wilbur Mentzer, waiting to go down the ladder. The two of us rushed down the ladder into the LVT hold. I was hurrying alongside one of the LVTs when I realized the one I was supposed to board was already off the deck.

All of a sudden a strong hand grabbed me firmly by the leg and a loud voice commanded, "Cunningham, get down here." It was First Sergeant Burgess pulling me down into his tractor. "You get right in here behind me, Cunningham. I might get hit and you'll be handy to take care of me."

I can still see those LVTs circling in formation while waiting for the signal to head in for the beach. Finally word came, and I watched on ahead as we got closer and closer to the beach. We landed rather smoothly and without any complications. I could not believe it was so hard to cross that beach going on up through that powdery volcanic ash. Was that ever tough! A short time later I learned the tractor I was to have boarded with Corporal Curtsinger took a direct hit going in. My first thought was that my God was watching over me.

Going in, the equipment I carried included a carbine, a .45

pistol, a backpack with a blanket roll, a K-bar, grenades, a medical kit with morphine syrettes, sulfa packets, battle dressings, and a canvas pack of surgical knives and scissors. Later I learned all that gear weighed fifty-one pounds. I don't think we had as many men wounded as the waves immediately following us.

A short time later Sgt. Bob Holmes and I were sheltered in a big shell hole just over the top. Another Marine walked to the edge of shell hole and spoke to Sgt. Holmes, who returned the greeting and added, "You better get down in here with us, John, where you'll have some cover."

John whoever it was replied, "I'm OK. Nothing's going to happen to me."

Afterward Sgt. Holmes told me the Marine was John Basilone, the hero of Guadalcanal who was cited with the Congressional Medal of Honor for his daring and courageous actions when he and Bob were fighting there. A short time later Gunnery Sergeant Basilone was killed as result of a direct hit by a mortar shell. How sad it was.

Later on I helped Sgt. Holmes get Japanese out of a cave. (I knew how to say "come here" in Japanese; we were instructed in a list of phrases learned when we were aboard ship coming from Hawaii.) Two Japs ran out of the cave back to front. Bob Holmes yelled, "Hit the deck!" We both dropped to the ground as they parted. Between them were strings that, as they ran from each other, triggered a grenade attached between them. It went off and killed both, but none of the shrapnel hit us.

During one firefight we were dug in on a knoll. Running between us and another platoon was a long path. I happened to look up and see a Marine from our platoon about fifty feet away running down the path. He was yelling as he ran because a series of mortar shells were following him. He knew they were meant for him. I ran over and tackled him and pulled him over to one side. Then I gave him a shot of morphine to calm him. I sent him back to the aid station. I think they took him to the beach instead. I chanced to run into him several years later back in the States. Neither of us mentioned the incident.

I remember treating Herb Schumacher for his wound. He asked me not to tell his brother. A few minutes later I went around to the other side of the hill to see another casualty. There was Ed Schumacher, freshly wounded. As I worked on him, he asked that I not tell his brother, Herb.

Several times a day, usually when I was taking care of a wounded Marine, one of our lieutenants came over to me with one excuse after another. He wanted me to send him on back to the hospital. After five or six days of that, I went to Sgt. Burgess and asked that he get the lieutenants off my back. Needless to say, that problem ended quickly.

I remember taking Ralph Baker back to the aid station. He was hit by multiple pieces of shrapnel. Dr. Brown told me to start suturing. While I was working on Ralph, he passed away.

Our company went back near the base of Mount Suribachi for a rest. Our platoon was told to send a squad of Marines and patrol around the east side of the hill. Our right guide, Sgt. Smallwood, six Marines, and I started out, with Smallwood on the point. I was next. After we went forward a hundred feet along the trail, Sgt. Smallwood warned us to freeze. The area we entered was a minefield. It seemed like hours, but it was probably a matter of several minutes that we stood there afraid to move. It also seemed that it took us hours to walk gingerly backward out of there, stepping in the tracks we made a short time before.

That night we were still in the rest area close to Suribachi. I could hear Japs crawling by our shell hole where we alternately slept and stood watch. I was told not to move. I did sleep with my trusty .45 in hand, holding it on my chest. I was thankful we had no trouble otherwise that night.

Corpsman Elmo Eastman of Easy Company was shot through the head when he went to help two Marines who shot each other in the foot so they would have to be evacuated immediately from battle. Another member of my platoon told me that he was not surprised by their cowardice, as they both cheated at cards.

A few days after returning to the front line from the "rest area," Fox Company was engaged in another firefight with the enemy. Jerry Cunningham was kneeling over a wounded man caring for him. A grenade came rolling over the ground toward Jerry. He had no time to do anything about it, even though he saw it coming. As it rolled beneath his abdomen, it exploded and ripped a huge laceration in his abdominal wall. He rose up to his knees, and glistening loops of bowel slithered through the laceration. He tried to stuff the loops back into his abdomen, but they only poured out faster. All at once whole kernel corn poured from a laceration in the bowel itself. He was evacuated from the site back to the aid station. At the time, I was caring for another corpsman with a similar abdominal wound caused by shrapnel. Dr. Collins checked Jerry and told another corpsman to pour in sulfa crystals, apply large battle dressings to the glistening extruded loops of bowel, pour saline solution on those and tie more large dry dressings over those. Chief Klinger returned and helped lift Jerry to an ambulance for transport back to one of the hospitals at the rear.

As Told by Thomas Brown, Lt. jg (MC), USNR:

Very early in the morning of February 19, 1945, the PA system of the LCI on which we were sailing from Saipan to Iwo Jima rudely, noisily awakened one and all with reveille. The cause of all the hurry was not apparent. We would not debark for several hours yet. Already, after only a few hours' sleep, my waking day was two hours old. The abrasive artificial chanticleer stirred me from my stretched canvas sack in the stuffy quarters that the Marine officers of 2-27 occupied and shoved me out on the path to the head, where I showered and shaved alongside others of our unit. Breakfast at the Officers' Mess was steak and eggs. To many of us it was like the last meal before our execution. We did not indulge in that special repast. Rather, we sat glumly drinking coffee and smoking cigarettes and exchanging scattered bits of conversation. In due time we returned to the sleeping quarters to check our packs, tighten helmet straps, fix blanket rolls, check items in the lower of our two backpacks, and take one last, fond look at the pictures of loved ones. After making a final check of our weapons and ammunition, we parked our bottom backpacks in a designated area of the deck just outside the hatch of our quarters and walked over to another hatch that opened to the deck below. There we climbed down a ladder, went over to our respective LVTs, climbed over the gunwales, and dropped to the deck of the landing vehicle to wait within until we were spewed out into the sea for that long ride to the snarling waiting beach.

At a given signal the ramp in the bow of the ship was unsecured, opened out into the bright sunlight, and lowered by its winches and chains to the surface of the glittering sea. Once out on the sparkling waves, the tractors gathered into organized groups of fixed numbers and churned like clock wheels in circular formations. Each group was a wave or a part of a wave appointed to land on a specific part of the beach at a specific moment. Each group churned in its own fixed circle until it was notified to move into its respective fixed line paralleling the beach a mile away. This was the line of departure and formed with respect to the command LVT, which was marked by a special flag and gave to each line the signal to depart. Each LVT in each line pointed its bow straight forward toward that fatal shore.

We were just a small part of a panorama that we surveyed during those moments of waiting. Many miles to the rear we saw long streaks of white flame shooting obliquely toward the sky from invisible battleships and cruisers lying beyond the horizon. A few seconds later we heard the roar of the charges propelling those

63

shells from their cannon on the ships' decks. They were supporting our landing with that mammoth bombardment of the island's surface. From our positions just above the surface of the ocean we watched explosion after explosion of those shells as they finished their missions by slamming against the east side of Suribachi. They blew great masses of dirt and boulders upward and outward to roll on down the hillside into the sea.

As our linear formation sped from the line of departure in toward the beach, those explosions on Suribachi became more and more spectacular. A filmy cloud of dust and smoke rose from the island as the conflict began in earnest. Flashes of gunfire shot out from enemy installations just above the shoreline. About two hundred yards or less offshore our gunboats and destroyers dashed along paths parallel to the beach as they returned fire toward the revealed enemy positions. We watched that Martian spectacle almost twenty-five minutes. Suddenly a dense cloud of very black smoke appeared over the island due to giant smoke bombs lobbed in to vaporize and conceal the initial assault waves from the crouched enemy. An observer plane flying well above the black cloud flamed brightly for a moment in its tail section. A black ribbon of smoke trailed from its back end as it curled over and headed downward with its pilot, his tour of duty ending in a crash somewhere in that pall ahead of us.

The coxswain yelled, "Everybody down!" Realizing we were almost at the target, we knelt on the deck and faced forward. As I looked across and toward the bow, I saw a machine-gunner kneeling with his heavy weapon across the back of his shoulders. He grinned back at me, giving me the thumbs-up sign of encouragement. His assistant, bearing a tripod for the gun, was just behind him. Just before we landed the coxswain called, "This is it, gang! Have a good day!" Exactly two minutes behind the second wave, we in the third rode that vehicle as it ground up onto the beach.

Someone lowered the ramp and we started pouring forward out over it. Following instructions, I looked for wounded. All the wounded I saw were dead. As did all of those ahead of me, I broke into a running trudge through that deep black sand. Suddenly I heard the voice of Roy Brown. His words were unintelligible in that din. I spotted him holding an unconscious Marine whose head was terribly wounded. Just as we finished applying a dressing to his head, the man died. On I went through that retarding sand and started up the escarpment to the top. A barrage of enemy artillery shells poured in on us. Those barrages were frightening to endure. The shellbursts came so fast and so close at hand that I had no time to worry between them. While I was eating a lot of sand, I rotated my head to the left and looked back across the black ocean. Another wave of LTVs was rumbling onto the beach. Behind it as far as I could see was our huge supporting flotilla. A profound feeling of loneliness gripped me despite those many Marines all around me. No one back home knew I was here on this gruesome beach. They were still sleeping or just arising. If I were to be killed, none would know it for several days. Even then they would not know exactly what had happened to me.

Eventually the two corpsmen and myself walked over to the nearby embankment of the first airfield. Turning left, we swung back along it in the direction of Suribachi, knowing that when we reached the corner of the airfield we could turn right and cross over to the west side of the island. Just as we passed that corner, our friends in the enemy artillery started blasting away at us again. When the barrage ended, we heard a voice calling for help. Two wounded Marines lay on the ground just thirty feet ahead of us. I instructed the two corpsmen to care for one, and I checked the other. He was dying from extensive shrapnel wounds. He was really ripped apart. For some reason I gave him a shot of morphine. He stopped breathing a minute or two afterward.

Those two corpsmen had learned well. By the time I joined them, one already had reconstituted a unit of dried plasma and started hanging it on the man's rifle, which was jammed muzzle-down into the ground. The second applied a battle dressing to a wounded leg, which he splinted. We placed the man on a litter and told his fellowmen to carry him down to the beach to be evacuated to a ship.

The three of us started south again. Standing in a foxhole before me was Lieutenant Kling, a platoon leader in the First Battalion, Twenty-seventh. Obviously we were not in our own territory. In response to my query as to the whereabouts of the front lines, he replied that they were up there where we took care of those two men. We moved on in a hurry. Lt. Kling was killed about twenty minutes later in another barrage. His brother was also a lieutenant and a platoon leader in Fox Company of our battalion.

On making our right turn toward the west side, we began "snooping and pooping" through scattered piles of dirt and rocks and also clumps of scraggly brush, crawling over the terrain or trotting in stooped postures. Suddenly one of the corpsmen grasped my arm while he whispered an alarm to wait. Forty feet straight ahead were three Japanese soldiers crouched on the ground in single file with rifles in hand, looking to the south. Fortunately, they had not heard us. We watched them a few minutes as they knelt silently. One of the corpsmen perceived that these Japanese did not seem to be breathing. Presuming them to be dead, we moved cautiously toward, but not to them. Perhaps they were booby-trapped. We did not understand what had killed them. There was not a mark of injury on any of them. Fifty or sixty feet beyond was a huge crater in the ground fifty feet wide and ten feet deep. One of the exploding sixteen-inchers must have done that. At a similar distance beyond the crater were five more of the enemy also transfixed in the same crouching position. While those two scenes were great demonstrations of the protective powers of our powerful weapons, they were stark testimony to the evil vicissitudes of conflicts such as this. But for the grace of God, the same destruction might have been heaped upon us. The rest of the crossing was uneventful.

Near the top of the crest of the west beach, I spotted Lt. Don Hendricks of Fox Company leaning against one of those primitive low-growth trees dotting the landscape. I asked him, too, of the whereabouts of the front lines. He sharply reprimanded me as he scolded, "Doc, you dumb ass, do you want to get your head blown off? What are you doing here, anyway? The First Platoon is up there just in front of us pinned down by one of those big Nambus [Japanese heavy machine guns]. So far we haven't been able to locate it. Now get your butt out of here and go on back to the battalion CP (command post) back near the beach where you belong. We really need you, Doc. Don't fool around up here and get yourself killed unnecessarily."

That was the last moment I ever saw Don alive. He was very, very likable. Several mornings later he was brought into another of our aid stations farther up the west side. He was pale and lifeless. In the center of his brow was a small bullet wound.

Needless to say, we did not backtrack across the island to look for the CP. We retreated about seventy-five yards to the rear, dug foxholes, and set up a miniature aid station. Three hours later the CP, which included the aid station in toto, came by, and we moved on forward a couple hundred yards. The First Platoon had long since found and destroyed the bunker stalling it and moved on. We dug more foxholes for the new position and set about organizing our first real aid station for action. The personnel manning it included Dr. Tom Collins, our senior medical officer; myself; Chief Pharmacist's Mate Milt Klinger of Chicago; Leon Hutchinson from somewhere in Michigan, a registered pharmacist; John Robert Long, also a registered pharmacist, from Mexico, Missouri; Bill Swank from Illinois; James Funk from Corvallis, Oregon; Jim White, the full-blooded hillbilly from the mountains of eastern Tennessee; and Ed Jones. The last six named were phar-macist's mates in the US Navy and, like myself, assigned to the Marine Corps by official order. Happily, the entire group survived the entire battle without serious wounds.

7

Bullet Wounds

Sergeant Smalley: Between the Eyes

While the Fifth Marine Division was still stationed at Camp Pendleton, Oceanside, California, the Marine Corps provided "bus" transportation from somewhere north of Laguna Beach to Camp Pendleton daily, except Sunday. We referred to that vehicle, which was a semi-trailer with board benches around the periphery of the inside walls, as "the Cattle Car." Those boarding at the start of the route usually sat well up front in order to avoid the bustle of later boarders or perhaps, to gain a few more winks of sleep en route.

Every morning when I was on duty at Pendleton, I left my dear wife, Adeline, at 5:30 A.M. and hastened along three blocks of down-sloping street to await the Cattle Car at the stop by the Oceanside Hotel on the west side of Route 1. Sometimes I sat next to Sgt. Carvil Smalley, who had served with the Marine Para-troopers in a number of Solomon Island assaults about a year or so before. One morning, in all his military wisdom, he assured me that Japanese soldiers could not shoot straight because of their slanted eyes. He was genuinely sincere during this discourse. Years later I learned that many Marines who served in the South Pacific had this same misgiving about the marksmanship of the Japanese. They must have obtained this misinformation from the same unreliable source. Unfortunately, Smalley was killed in the

69

battle at Iwo Jima. Afterward, back at Camp Tarawa on the island of Hawaii, I inquired of one of his buddies about Sergeant Smalley's death.

"He was standing in his foxhole when a sniper fired at him," his buddy told me. "He heard a bullet zing above his head.

" 'Down four!' Smalley defiantly shouted. Again the sniper fired and missed.

" 'Down two!' the arrogant sergeant called."

His buddy continued, "The next shot caught Smalley right between the eyes and killed him."

Why such men stubbornly had faith in this mistaken belief I don't know. It certainly didn't stem from a reasonable intellectual process. Human eyes are much the same despite races and pigmentation and any anatomical features peculiar to one's ethnic origin. Bravery unaccompanied by normal astuteness or knowledge or reason is sometimes a treacherous enemy.

Kill Him Again!

The intensity of emotions in battle—emotions such as fear, hatred, anxiety, disgust, and horror—may traumatize one's psyche. This is particularly true when the trauma is continuous minute after minute, hour after hour, and day after day as it was at Iwo Jima. A sustained potpourri of emotional stresses incites instant, uncontrolled, surprising reactions that we may look back upon in disbelief, wonderment, or disgust. "Why did I do that?" a soldier might ask. That question crops up among combat veterans when recalling unusual, exciting experiences.

The following anecdote was related by Corpsmen Les Murrah and Ray Hansen independently. They were assigned to the same forty-man platoon in Easy Company and were foxhole buddies one dark night during the battle. Murrah was standing an alternate two-hour watch. As he peered through the darkness beyond their foxhole, he spied a figure crawling in his direction. He quickly seized his carbine and waited as the Japanese soldier crawled slowly, stealthily, ever nearer. Murrah's heart raced as he waited for the enemy to get into a position at which he could shoot. Just as the assailant rose upward to a crouching position to jump into their hole, Murrah fired a bullet into his chest. The shot aroused Hansen, who heard someone ask, "Who's there?" At that moment a star shell burst above.

Hansen saw the silhouette of a second enemy soldier about to jump into his foxhole. It replied in a garbled voice, trying to say, "It's me." Hansen quickly grabbed his semifolded trenching shovel while thrusting his leg and foot up in the air to offset the intruder. The assailant put a hammer lock on Hansen's foot and leg, which he apparently mistook for Hansen's head and neck. Hansen pulled his leg back, and the enemy came with it. With wild abandonment Hansen pulled the blade up to a ninety-degree angle with respect to the handle and began mercilessly pounding the enemy. Meanwhile Murrah unwittingly stood on the second invader's head looking forward for more enemy soldiers. Hansen started kicking wildly with his free leg as the enemy hung on. He shouted to Murrah to shoot the assailant. He complied, firing down between his feet into the man's head. Murrah watched in amazement and finally said, "What on earth are you doing, Hansen?"

"I'm killing him," explained Hansen as he continued to pummel the corpse.

"But I've already killed him," said a bewildered Murrah sharply.

"I know it, Les," said Ray as he swung again at the enemy. "I'm killing him again before he kills one of us," Hansen explained illogically as he added a few more blows. The hammerlock hold relaxed. Perhaps Hansen's reaction was provoked by stories he had heard from old-timers about the enemy in other Pacific battles who simulated death, then treacherously and wildly attacked U.S. troops who came near.

71

In a letter to Keith Nielson dated 11/2/92, Ray Hansen commented:

I remember the night a Jap came into my foxhole. Three of us were in it, me, Murrah, and Sergeant Carr. We drew straws for the first one off. I drew the short one. We each had a .45 caliber pistol. Carr had a carbine, too. I loaned my .45 to Lt. Kellogg. I was just about asleep when I heard someone say, "It's me." Then the shooting began.

It was just about dark. I looked up and saw someone coming in. I put my right leg up to stop him. The Jap grabbed my foot and put a hammer lock on my leg. He must have thought it was my head. I lowered my leg and the Jap with it. Murrah stepped up on the Jap's head, looking around for more intruders. Meanwhile I kicked like the devil to get free and yelled at Murrah to shoot him.

Murrah said, "He's dead, Hansen, he's dead."

I said, "Shoot the S.O.B." My foot was right under the Jap's head as Murrah stood on it. Murrah put his .45 between his feet and shot him. Lucky for me, the bullet did not go all the way through his head. When the Jap came in our foxhole, Carr jumped out. Anyway, Murrah and I had to throw the body out. Murrah's hands shook for a long time. In the morning I found a Japanese hand grenade one foot away from my head. It was a concussion grenade that landed in the soft dirt, so there was not enough impact to detonate it or I wouldn't be here now. I still have the grenade.

As far as the rest of the night was concerned, there was no rest. The Japs got someone a few hours later. One of the Marines made it to our foxhole. I patched him up. He told us the other man in his foxhole was so badly wounded he wouldn't make it. He told us not to go after him. I can still hear him calling for "Rags," our code word for corpsman, for about an hour after that. It seemed like forever. In the morning, I went over to the hole and saw how bad he was. Nothing on our part would have helped. I also went on to Hoffman's foxhole and saw the job the Japs did on him and his buddy. I think the sword you have is the one they used on Hoffman.

On September 19, 1992, in a letter to Walter O'Malley, another Easy Company stalwart on Iwo, Keith Neilsen wrote a bit of history from his memory of the same event just described:

The way I remember, it was the end of the day after taking the last ridge in the charge led by Lieutenant Lummus. About forty of us were left in Easy Company. We were on the last lip of high ground digging in for the night, and the Japs were in caves just over the edge and back under us. Just before dark, two persons walked in from the right. Murrah called, "Who's there?"

The semi-intelligible answer, "It's me. It's me," was rather difficult to understand. At that instant a star flare popped above us and lit up the area. We saw they were Japs. One froze and crouched down. The other ran to jump in the foxhole with Murrah and Hansen. Murrah shot him with his .45. The Jap landed across Murrah's lap and grabbed Hansen's leg. Hansen beat him with his trenching shovel while shouting, "Shoot him again, Murrah." I popped the other one.

A few days later, after the Japs jumped in with our corpsmen, some other Japs got someone down at the left end of the line. The Marine screamed, "Rags, please help me," all night. We knew the Japs captured him, so the corpsmen stayed in their holes. About 0300 the Japs killed Sergeant Harris and knifed Hoffman. A little later, they killed Hoffman. A Jap got in Morris' hole and pitched a hand grenade at me. It landed under the muzzle of my rifle, blew shrapnel into my fingers when it exploded and blew dirt in my eyes. When the same Jap tried to come on in, O'Brovac got him.

Author's Note: Here we have three accounts of the same incidents. Similarities and mild dissimilarities are noted. The reports were written in good faith and following time lapses. Hectic activities such as these were burned indelibly in our minds. Perhaps the darkness and the frenzied action of close-in battle are more responsible, in the main, for the variations in these accounts.

How a Goldbrick Saved My Life

When we reported in for duty at the Fifth Marine Division about March 1, 1944, Dr. Charles Hely and I were assigned to the Twenty-Seventh Regiment, where we quickly took over the command and operation of its Sick Bay. We were endowed with the title of Regimental Surgeon. At last someone had recognized how talented we were and positioned us where our abilities would be properly used! Two weeks later superior rank moved in: Charley became the doctor for the Third Battalion and I for the Second. Yet for one short moment we were in our glory as regimental surgeons.

Early on in that two weeks it became obvious to us that the regiment was strongly victimized by a plague of sore feet and bad backs. Most of those bad feet and backs belonged to "goldbricks," our terminology for fakers. So Charley and I rose to the occasion with the original practice of "Second Opinion." When I had seen a man from our own respective battalion two or three times for the same minor complaint and reached the conclusion that there was no real physical basis for the complaint, I would tell my patient that I wished for him to be examined by Dr. Hely for a second opinion. Likewise, my fellow doctor would send his goldbricks over to me. From our standpoint, it was a good system. One big, strapping Marine was referred to Dr. Hely by me. After a few minutes of a good examination I heard Charley say in his best gruff voice, "Mac, there's not a confounded thing wrong with you. You are an excellent physical specimen and in good health. You're nothing but a goldbrick. Now, get your butt out of here and don't ever come back again unless you're *really* sick or need an immunization." The young private's jaw dropped as he hurriedly slunk out of that Twenty-seventh Sick Bay. Until that day we were seeing over ninety men at each of those two-a-day sick calls. To my amazement, after this incident, attendance at sick call dropped off sharply.

D-Day arrived and as soon as our tractor hit the beach I

looked for wounded needing medical help. Since all the wounded I saw upon landing were dead, I hastily plodded across that beach of deep, black sand at a slow trudge and started up the escarpment. A barrage of artillery shells screamed in, so I hit the deck and started eating sand. After a couple minutes the barrage ceased. While I was lying there, a piece of shrapnel dropped out of space, its momentum spent, and hit my left thumb. This produced a little bleeding, but the wound was insignificant. With the cessation of shelling, I backed down to the bottom of the escarpment and looked about. About fifty yards to the right was a battered blockhouse perched at the top of a gully. Recognizing this blockhouse to be a good aid station, I crawled up and sat a few feet below it. As I turned to beckon to the two corpsmen standing below, I noticed small bits of dirt spitting out of the right side of the gully near me. Why would anyone want to kill me? I had never hurt anyone. That thought expired in about ten seconds as it became obvious to me that the enemy was trying to eliminate me. The corpsmen saw the firing and wisely concluded it might be best to stay where they were. As I sat there in the gully, I tried to determine if they had seen me or were just firing in my direction. So I used the age-old deceptive maneuver of raising my helmet on my rifle's muzzle. *Ping! Ping!* My question was immediately answered. They hit the helmet all right but couldn't quite get down to it when it rested on my head.

A Marine rifleman passing by well to my right saw that bit of action. He bravely walked to the side of the only door of the blockhouse and tossed in two grenades. After the dust and smoke cleared, he looked in, then grinned my way and called, "I got three of the bastards, Doc!" He got his first enemy and saved my life in the process. I looked up at him in gratitude. It was the goldbrick we had kicked out of Sick Bay! Being called that name had helped him to become a first-class Marine. He went through the entire battle of Iwo Jima without a scratch.

Sgt. Wilbur Burgess

First Sgt. Wilbur Burgess was a red-headed, stocky, fiery, battle-hardened Raider. He was an affable man, but he made frequent appearances at our Sick Bay at Camp Tarawa complaining of sore feet and a paining back. He was a noisy sort of guy, and the troops serving him enjoyed his boisterous, garish humor. They also had much respect for his instruction. One afternoon on our voyage to Saipan on the troopship, USS *Highlands,* we chanced to meet topside. He greeted me with, "Doc, back there in camp I was just goldbricking when I complained about my back and feet. To be honest, I didn't want to make this operation, but you were too smart for me, and I didn't get surveyed out of this outfit!"

In battle, Burgess was wounded, shot in the face by a bullet. He was evacuated from the front to the Fifth Division Station Hospital well to the rear. In early April 1945, our ship pulled into Pearl Harbor as we were en route to Hawaii and Camp Tarawa. While we were docked there, Major Antonelli told me to visit the Aiea Heights Hospital, a USN facility near the port, and check on troops of our battalion who might be there convalescing from wounds incurred on Iwo. Having finished the task, I was about to leave when who should come stomping down the hall toward me but old Burgess, sucking beer through a straw. The bullet had damaged or ruined altogether some of his teeth. Consequently, the dental surgeons had wired his teeth in fixed positions so he couldn't eat anything other than liquids sipped through a straw. Yet he was one happy Marine! He knew he would not make another operation, he was through with combat, and he was quite happy with his diet, mostly beer, sipped through a straw.

Don Sealye

Boxing was a form of both entertainment and sport with some Marines when in camp. Don Sealye of Dog Company was a very husky and muscular man who had quit in his senior year of high school to enlist with the Corps. Don loved to box. He boxed frequently during off-time hours, and usually he won. Iwo was a different kind of contest, though. He was unconscious as he was brought into our open-air aid station on a stretcher. His left eye had been hopelessly destroyed by a bullet. He was pale and in shock, with a very low blood pressure. It appeared certain that his brain must have been severely damaged by the bullet. There was no exit wound. One corpsman placed a dressing over the eye. Another attempted to start a unit of plasma intravenously. He was having much difficulty because the vein had collapsed. I took the needle and went for a deeper vein. Fortunately, it entered satisfactorily. That unit was then allowed to flow in rapidly. A second unit followed the first at a slower flow rate, and we shipped him on back to the Fifth Division hospital. We didn't have much hope for him.

At a Fifth Marine Division Association reunion in Chicago several years later I was taken aback by Don's surprising appearance. He was wearing the same wide, warm smile he had back in Camp Tarawa, but above it was a triangular black eye patch. Sticking my right hand forward toward his, I smirked. "Don, you're dead! You're not supposed to be here."

Shaking my hand with his own hand, which was twice the size of mine, he laughed and retorted, "I know it, Doc. I came just to spite you! I heard everything you said back in that aid station on Iwo. I was so stunned by the wound and the shock that I just couldn't talk. I heard everything, though. The corpsman couldn't get that plasma started, and every stick caused me a sharp pain. I heard you say, 'Give me that damn needle and I'll get it started. We've got to get him out of here and back to the hospital right away.' You did both. At the Navy hospital the doctors told me that the bullet ricocheted around in the bony orbit and back out again. Thanks for saving my life."

I don't think that we did, but we helped along the way. The bones forming the socket of the eye are paper thin. Apparently, the high velocity of the missile and the angle at which it struck must have been such that in a split second the bullet ricocheted around and out.

The Sounds of Bullets

As I recall, his name was Seal or Seals. He was seen in the battalion Sick Bay infrequently because of a purulent foul-smelling drainage in the external ear canals. We treated them by swabbing with a 10 percent solution of trichloracetic acid. The therapy was effective in clearing the drainage, but it always recurred. Today this affliction is known as "swimmer's ear."

Prior to shipping out for Iwo Jima, I received a letter from his mother expressing great concern that because of the ear infections his hearing might be impaired and he would be in jeopardy because of that impairment. She was worried that he would not be able to hear bullets in battle. Outwardly he manifested no evidence of impaired hearing, so we referred him to an otologist (ear specialist) at the AUS (Army of United States) Station Hospital a few miles from Camp Tarawa. Seals returned with a written report from the consultant. It stated that following a thorough examination of Seal's ears, it was the doctor's opinion that the drainage issued from a fungus infection of the external ear canals. He found no evidence of hearing impairment. Ed Jones, our recorder, typed a copy of the report concerning the examination. This was placed in Seals's hands, and he was instructed to send it to his mother in his next letter home.

Among the old "salts" of battle, it was a general opinion that

My wife and I at Laguna Beach, California, after being married only two weeks.

Pfc. Billy Menges stationed at Camp Pendleton in 1944.

WESTERN UNION

NEWCOMB CARLTON
CHAIRMAN OF THE BOARD

J. C. WILLEVER
FIRST VICE-PRESIDENT

1290

The filing time shown in the date line on telegrams and day letters is STANDARD TIME at point of origin. Time of receipt is STANDARD TIME at point of destination

LONG C9 78 GOVT=WASHINGTON DC 21 129A

1945 MAR 21 AM 3 32

LAURENCE LUCAL BROWN=

1815 WEST CHARLES MN=

THE NAVY DEPARTMENT DEEPLY REGRETS TO INFORM YOU THAT YOUR
BROTHER LIEUTENANT (JG) THOMAS MARTIN BROWN USNR HAS BEEN
WOUNDED IN ACTION WHILE IN THE SERVICE OF HIS COUNTRY. THE
DEPARTMENT APPRECIATES YOUR GREAT ANXIETY BUT EXTENT OF
WOUNDS NOT NOW AVAILABLE AND DELAY IN RECEIPT OF DETAILS
MUST NECESSARRILY BE EXPECTED BUT WILL BE FURNISHED YOU
PROMPTLY IF RECEIVED. TO PREVENT POSSIBLE AID TO OUR ENEMIES
PLEASE DO NOT DIVULGE THE NAME OF HIS SHIP OR STATION=

VICE ADMIRAL RANDALL JACOBS
CHIEF OF NAVAL PERSONNEL.

(JG).

Standard telegram announcing Lt. Thomas Martin Brown as wounded.

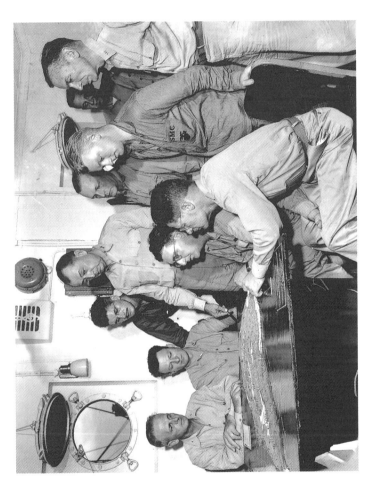

SUSMC and USN officers aboard a ship at a briefing session prior to the assault on Iwo Jima.

Waves of amphibious tractors streaking toward the beaches of Iwo Jima as they transport USMC assault forces.

Troops of Second Battalion, Twenty-seventh Marines, having crossed Red Beach-One, moving up the escarpments and over the top.

A marine rifleman moving forward over a ridge as comrades protect him with covering fire.

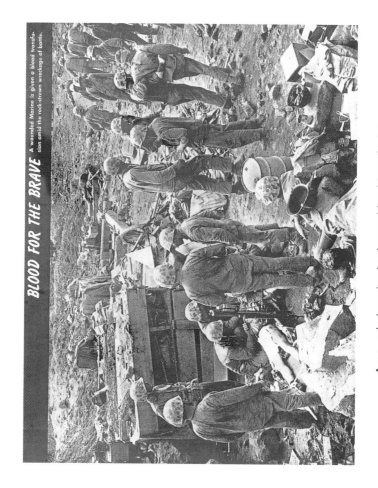

BLOOD FOR THE BRAVE A wounded Marine is given a blood transfusion amid the rock-strewn wreckage of battle.

A wounded marine is given a blood transfusion.

• • • AND THE LIVING Corpsmen carry a wounded Marine toward an evacuation boat while his comrades huddle in foxhole.

Corpsmen carry a wounded marine toward an evacuation boat.

CARE FOR THE WOUNDED Wounded Marines are placed aboard a pontoon barge awaiting removal to a hospital ship.

Wounded marines on a pontoon barge, awaiting removal to a hospital ship.

Part of an assault platoon in defilade, awaiting orders from headquarters to move out.

A very busy USMC machine gun crew in action.

Chief Klinger and I "dining out" on Iwo enjoying gourmet rations.

Capt. King and author standing near an aid station on D+21

A group of Red Cross volunteers, young ladies of Edwardsburg, Michigan, honored at a banquet for their many hours of labor at making rolls of gauze bandages and battle dressings to be used in actual battles.

A Japanese decoy, a dummy bunker emplacement to lure USMC troops into the line of their own machine gun fire.

Left to right: Lt. Jack Lummus, the subject of the story "Death of a Hero", striding in the background. In the middle is the author, and at right, Lt. Don Hendricks. Both Lummus and Hendricks were killed in action. This photo was taken in the officer's tent area at Camp Tarawa, USMC training camp, in a desert in the northern part of the Island of Hawaii. The photo was snapped about 2–3 months before we went into battle.

the bullets heard were passing by; however, those bullets that wounded were, by the victim, never heard.

Seals was killed in battle by a bullet through the head. His mother's concern was not minimized by me; I understood. Sadly enough, many a mother is subjected to the tragedy of losing a son in battle. However, Seals never could have been surveyed from military service because of that type of ear problem. I am sure that she never forgave me.

First Sergeant Harper

First Sgt. Esmond Harper walked in unattended and on his own power from a hot firefight in midafternoon. He had been in a semicrouched position giving orders to his men when he was drilled in the abdomen. The entry wound was a small, bloody hole in the skin just above the center of the pubic bone. The blood was clotted and nothing else exuded from it. That site of entry of the bullet made me suspect particularly the possibility of a penetrating wound of the urinary bladder. Sure enough, there was an irregular exit wound precisely opposite in the midline of the back in the lower lumbar area. He did not complain and did not appear in any way uncomfortable. He was a husky, leathery, tough ex-Raider of the type who would rather choke on pain than complain of it.

On beginning my examination I queried, "Sarge, does it hurt?" Urine that escapes from the bladder into the abdominal cavity can irritate the peritoneal lining of the cavity, causing excruciating pain. Yet he exhibited no sign of acute distress. That indeed was most puzzling.

"No, sir," he informed me. "There is no discomfort except where the bullet hit me. That area is sore, but not necessarily what I would call painful."

Further examination included listening over the abdomen with a stethoscope in searching for abnormal bowel sounds. There

95

were none, so the gut apparently hadn't been damaged, either. In addition, there was no pain or tenderness in any part of the abdomen when I applied pressure with my fingers. Also, the abdomen was not distended.

After I had ruminated and contemplated for a few minutes in search of an explanation for the lack of misery, the light dawned! Only one explanation existed. The bullet must have entered at any angle other than ninety degrees, deflected off the very top surface of the pubic bone, and subsequently ricocheted around his lower trunk in the planes between muscles or between the muscles and connective tissue. My hunch was correct. On striking the tough ligamentous tissue attached to the spinal column at the midline of the spinous processes of each vertebra, the bullet was immediately deflected through soft tissue and skin exactly 180 degrees opposite the entrance to make its exit from the body.

At first I wasn't very astute, being hung up on the mystifying absence of pain. But it was a rather circuitous, interesting, and not very disabling course the bullet had taken. We dressed his wound and sent him by ambulance on back to the Fifth Division Hospital to the rear.

Ebbtide and Flow

Some years ago on learning I was a veteran of the battle for Iwo Jima, a patient of mine informed me that her husband also fought in that operation as a member of the Fourth Marine Division. She was invited to bring him along at her next visit, if that might be convenient. As I perceived it, the occasion would offer me an opportunity to discuss experiences with a member of a division other than the Fifth. Their name was Byrd, and they lived in Saratoga, Indiana, a small town about thirty miles east of Muncie and a little north, in nearby Randolph County. He accompanied her on her next appointment two months later. His battalion had landed on Blue Beach Two, beneath those cliffs overlooking the entire east coast south to Suribachi.

During the first few days of battle, parts of the Fourth Marine Division were pinned down by heavy fire from enemy positions on the cliffs. This was particularly true of Byrd's battalion, which was immediately adjacent to the cliffs. On its left flank was some kind of a damaged, beached, small, Japanese boat. Every attempt by the immobile Marines to move forward from that situation was thwarted by devastating enemy fire resulting in heavy casualties. All at once the tide of battle changed, and the Marines moved swiftly forward. Byrd explained the abrupt change in rather simple terms.

After spending three days in the same foxhole, an astute observer noted that enemy fire increased when the tide ebbed and subsided when it flowed into the beach. An officer in charge commanded a watch be kept on the only porthole visible on the near side of the small beached boat. Tide was in at the moment, and action was light. After the tide refluxed into the ocean, a figure was seen moving inside the vessel past the porthole toward the stern end. Three sharpshooters were assigned to keep their sights fixed on the port and shoot anything moving by it.

Byrd was one of the sharpshooters assigned to the watch. When the water started rolling up the beach again, each one flipped off the safety of his rifle and waited and waited and waited. At last a head and chest were spotted as the man moved by the porthole. All three marksmen fired simultaneously. Thereafter the alternating intensity of fire stopped. Investigation of the interior of the boat revealed a radio set, including a transmitter, in the stern. The man was walking back and forth with the ebb and flow. When the tide was out he transmitted specific information about positions of the Marines and other pertinent data. Until then firing at the Marines was like shooting fish in a barrel. The tide of the battle changed when the tide of the ocean did and the transmitter of information made one trip too many past the port.

The Tragedy of Elmo Eastman

Elmo Eastman was thirty-five years of age when he hit the beach. A year before, he had come into our unit of 2-27. Elmo had left a wife and two small children at home when he enlisted. He was a very mature man and was also a stabilizing influence on the younger corpsmen and an excellent man to have working in the Sick Bay of our Second Battalion. He had a broad, warm, smile contagiously radiating from his mien to those about him. Above that was a head of thick, wavy black hair. He was very muscular and upright. Like many others in the Fifth Division, he asked for a transfer into an assault company six weeks before we left for battle. Some of the men in headquarters company, cooks, communications men, clerks, corpsmen, and men in the quartermaster's supply section, feeling a noble urge as the day of combat came closer, requested a change of assignments to assault companies. Some of the more venturesome probably desired a taste of glory. Elmo landed in the first wave with many Marines of his platoon.

A Marine who witnessed the whole scene described it to me as follows: "Shortly after landing in the first wave and running a few steps forward, two Marines faced one another, then each shot the other in a foot. They then loudly shouted, 'Corpsman.' The intent of the act was to wound and disable one another in order to become immediate casualties and be evacuated from combat as wounded in order to quickly reach safety early in the battle. As Elmo ran in response to that call, he was drilled through the head by an enemy bullet. We lost a very good corpsman in the very first few minutes of battle. Those two chicken hearts were evacuated to some ship for treatment."

Early in June 1945, after returning to Camp Tarawa, our battalion held a dress parade of all able-bodied men. Our commanding officer, now a colonel, stood well out in front of the battalion, all of the men being at attention. He then announced various medals and citations awarded in recognition for deeds of heroism, courage, and other commendable actions in the battle, by both individuals and units. Many personnel were notified of promotions in that same ceremony.

As the dress parade seemingly ended, Colonel Antonelli ordered two men behind the formation to march forward through the ranks and stand at attention six paces in front facing him. They were the two men who had disappeared from sight the past three months, the two who had inflicted the gunshot wounds in each other's feet. As they faced our commanding officer, they were dressed in green dungarees without the usual markings on their uniforms. A single eight-inch letter *P* marked the back of each jacket—Prisoner. The colonel commanded, "About face," and proceeded to proclaim aloud, "Each of you has been court-martialed for an act of cowardice in the face of enemy fire and found guilty. You are hereby sentenced to fifteen years of hard labor in a U.S. Navy correctional facility and to receive a dishonorable discharge from the U.S. Marine Corps." It was a sad day, first to be reminded of Elmo and second to observe the official disgracing of the Marine Corps by those two men.

In a copy of his *Memoirs of Iwo Jima,* which Jerry Cunningham sent me in 1993, I found this note: "Elmo Eastman, Ph M 1/C, was killed by a bullet through the head when he went to help two Marines, ——— and ———, who were calling for a corpsman. I found out they shot each other in the foot in order to get off the island. I told a member of our platoon the story. He said it did not surprise him, as those two also cheated at cards."

To Arms, Two Arms

Sgt. Nolan Garrett was a small, tough, shrewd, animated ex-Paratrooper from somewhere in Texas. He and Sergeant Smalley were buddies from way back. Garrett was a fatalist with regard to the hour of his death. Unlike Smalley, he had no misgivings about the marksmanship of the Japanese. He was also somewhat of a philosopher. Because of his fatalism, he was fearless in his action in battle, believing that if his hour came, it came. If not, then he would be unharmed.

One day he walked nonchalantly into our aid station from the zone of an ongoing battle. He sought attention for a wound in his left shoulder, a bullet having pierced the bulky part of his shoulder laterally and passed on through it. There was no obvious impairment of muscular function, fortunately. As soon as we had cleaned and sterilized the wound, sprinkled it with sulfa crystals, and bandaged it, he thanked us, grabbed his carbine, and headed back up front to his outfit and his duty.

A few days later Garrett again walked into our aid station, this time accompanied by his platoon corpsman. Both were members of Dog Company. Again Garrett had been wounded by a bullet, but this time it was in the right wrist. His position, squatting on the front deck of a tank just before the turret as he pointed out to the crew where to fire, made him a prime target for a sniper. His company, supported by tanks, was pushing forward against the obstinate enemy. As he pointed to a target with his outstretched hand and finger, a bullet entered the lateral, or "pinky," side of his wrist anteriorly and emerged just below the right thumb at its palmar aspect.

No active bleeding from the new wound in the right wrist was evident. He could extend fully the digits of the right hand to a straightforward posture and flex them forward to the palm. Certainly one might suspect the wrist would be damaged by a bullet passing through in that region. It was not. That bullet must have been rapidly deflected by certain bones and tendons so that it passed harmlessly, amazingly, among the many tendons, ligaments, blood vessels, and nerves without causing any destruction. When we finished dressing the entrance and exit wounds of the bullet's path, we checked for any other sign of impairment, then inspected the shoulder wound. Inspection and evaluation revealed that redressing was not necessary. After we finished, he again thanked us, picked up his carbine and headed once more for the battlefront. He suffered no further injuries during the remainder of the battle.

Stories of Paul Bradford

Paul Bradford, a corpsman in Fox Company, described a case of one of his platoon, injured in battle, who incurred a bullet wound with entry in the right side of the neck. Paul spotted an obvious exit wound beneath the left eye. The mouth and nose of the injured man were not involved, nor was there evidence of any impairment elsewhere. One can only speculate what unusual path that bullet had traveled in reaching the site of emergence. Possibly it coursed behind the skull or vertebral column to deviate under the ear and bounce off the left mandible (jawbone) and then upward obliquely under soft tissues to its exit site.

*　　*　　*

Bradford also attended a Marine in the front lines who had held his right arm upright to give a signal to his comrades. On doing so, he was shot in the right axilla (armpit) and the missile emerged through the skin surface of the left abdomen just below the bottom rib. Paul quickly ran to attend the injured man. Sadly, he died in the corpsman's arms shortly afterward. The bullet must have taken a circuitous route and been deflected by bony structures through the aorta or heart. A massive hemorrhage or cardiac arrest ensued to account for the quick demise.

*　　*　　*

On another occasion, two litter bearers carried another wounded man back to Paul at the platoon area. Paul administered a syrette of morphine and accompanied him on back to our battalion aid station. Outwardly he appeared to be in favorable condition except for a ragged exit wound in the skin of the neck about one inch below the angle of the jaw. He complained to us of pain in the right side of his chest. His fatigue jacket was unbuttoned and laid open. We then pulled up his green skivvy shirt and were quite surprised to see a small, unremarkable entry wound in the lateral aspect of the right side of his thorax, for his complaint with regard to that pain was minimal. The skin immediately around the entry wound bore a bluish discoloration as though it had been contused. No other damage was apparent. The bullet causing his complaint must have been deflected upward by an underlying rib right after it had pierced the skin. It passed over the next five ribs and on up under the clavicle (collarbone) en route to its exit in the neck. Only muscle in the side of the neck prevented it from traveling a more destructive path through vital blood vessels and nerves.

We sprinkled sulfadiazine crystals in the wounds, applied new dry dressings, put more information on his red tag, and told him we were shipping him back to the hospital. He hastily sat up and asked, "It won't take long, will it, Doc? I need to get back up to my outfit."

Truly this man was committed to his fellow Marines.

Colonel Plain

Col. Louis Plain was the executive officer of our Twenty-seventh Regiment. He served as one of the Old Corps of Marines who were on active duty for years before World War II even started. He had participated in conflicts in the banana republics of South America back in the 1920s as well as more recent ones in the South Seas of the Pacific. He was a huge man of six-five or -six in stature. He was solid as a rock. Combat Marine duty was his dish. He was gruff in manner and voice, very officious and concise in his commands, but a realistic and considerate officer beneath it all. His mannerisms were to him a way to get things done. He loved being in command.

At the end of the artillery barrage that pinned me to the up-slope of the far side of Red Beach One, I arose to my feet and looked to the right for some kind of shelter for an aid station. As I scanned the crest of that slope off to the right, I spotted the unmistakable figure of Colonel Plain walking fearlessly along the crest of that slope waving that huge right arm and apparently shouting commands to someone as he moved along. The noise of all the explosions and bursts of gunfire was music to his ears, but it drowned out his voice. Later I was told that early in the battle a bullet shattered one elbow and took him out of action. That large waving extremity certainly made a wonderful target. I never learned the explicit details of his wounding.

He was evacuated to the beach, I presume, for the Fifth Division Hospital was not established ashore until at least D+4. From the beach he was transported to a ship. Eventually he was treated in a base hospital back in the States. The elbow joint was ruined. It was deformed and stiff. As a result he was relegated to a desk job in Washington, D.C., for the rest of his active career in the USMC. Being a devotee of action, he was miserably frustrated, but still very much alive. The effects of battle wounds are many, and the variable ways they rudely change the courses of human lives are unpredictable.

Glen Daugherty

Glen Daugherty was one of the U.S. Navy corpsmen assigned to the medical section of Hq. Co. 2-27. He reported into our Sick Bay about mid-May or June 1944. He was reared in Alexandria, Indiana, a small town twelve miles west and a little north of Muncie. The bloom of youth was still on his cheeks when he joined our outfit. He was a year out of high school. We were both avid basketball addicts, but he was a far more accomplished athlete than I. Basketball was a common ground for conversation between us. For all practical purposes we were Hoosier neighbors. The bugler of our Second Battalion was a Marine named Jack Wright. His hometown was Summitville, Indiana, a farm community five miles northeast of Alexandria. He and Glen had been contemporaries in different high schools. As opponents they had waged many a hard-fought game in their student days. They became fast friends off the court, and on graduation from high school they went together to enlist, one in the U.S. Marine Corps the other in the U.S. Navy. Glen left behind a high school sweetheart named Wanda when he left for active duty.

A few weeks before we shipped out from Camp Pendleton, Glen consulted me about a three day weekend liberty, so he and Wanda might be wed before we left the States. My self-contained reaction was they should wait until he returned from overseas. But remembering my own recent nuptials, I consented and requested a three-day pass from Major Antonelli for Glen.

"Give him five," the major instructed. "We don't know whether he will return, nor whether you or I will, for that matter."

Censoring letters of the enlisted men of one's command was an unwanted duty heaped on young officers. Some of our corpsmen requested their mail pass through my censorship. In a postbattle letter written to my wife in early April 1945, I commented about Glen's letters to Wanda. Perhaps that was because of empathy. Each began: "My Dearest, Darling Wanda, how I love you and long for you. I wish we were together tonight." My throat tightened as I wrote . On D+4, Glen rushed to the absolute front to attend a wounded comrade of his platoon and was immediately killed by machine-gun fire that caught him in the chest.

In mid-January 1946, while on a thirty-day leave, I drove to Alexandria in a very blustery snowstorm to visit Glen's parents. His father was away at work. Glen's mother greeted me. She told

104

me she had cancer of the breast, which had spread randomly through her body. She was in a lingering process of dying. She was very embittered because she would never see her son again. Her rancor was exacerbated because a short time before, Glen's widow, Wanda, had married their mutual friend from high school days, Jack Wright. Glen's mother was emotionally wounded because Wanda did not wait a few months longer, as if that would give her some peace of mind. In my own opinion, as a great authority on marital problems, Glen was long gone. He was the type who would have heartily approved that second marriage of Wanda's, given the circumstances. Who else would better care for her and love her and treat her with more respect?

During the return trip to Muncie, the intensity of the snowstorm increased to such a level that visibility was impaired. The highway was slick and treacherous. Between the snowstorm and Mrs. Daugherty's vitriolic words, I was moved to regret that I had ever made that trip. Her emotions were understandable. But my own postbattle reactions were still quite volatile.

A Case of Pork and Beans

Jim Huddleston of Muncie, Indiana, and formerly of 2-28 related the following bit of history as the absolute, sworn truth. His wife, who was not with him at the time of this revelation of history, independently verified his statements at a later date and alleged that he had related the story to her as absolutely true after he returned home from overseas. This is his story:

Following the capture of Mt. Suribachi, our regiment reorganized and headed north to join other elements of the Fifth Division in the savage struggle to capture the rest of the island. This was a few days after we had raised our red, white, and blue above the hill. Our squad was sitting in foxholes waiting for the order to move out to destroy a bunker a short distance ahead of our platoon. It was a formidable installation and had been a difficult obstacle for our company the past few hours. We sat and sat in those foxholes leaning back against the hot, volcanic soil for the longest time. An hour must have passed before the order to move out finally arrived.

We were so bored with sitting there leaning back against the hot earth, we were ready to go the second the order arrived. Our helmets were strapped, carbines loaded with safeties off and lying across our laps, and packs on our backs. We all jumped out and started running forward in squad formation. Some were firing away as they ran, some were throwing grenades as others covered with protective fire. We anticipated crossfire, but none like what we received. They were waiting for us and gave us a warm welcome.

As I ran, the enemy fire seemed to be coming from all directions. I went forward about twenty-five yards when something hit me in the back real hard and knocked me over on the ground. I fell so hard my breath was knocked out of me. As I fell, I knew I had been hit, but didn't know how badly. As I lay there face down on the ground, something warm began oozing over the back of my chest where I was hit. I yelled, "Corpsman!" as loudly as I could. "I've been hit," I screamed through all the noise and chaos.

A voice replied, "I'll be there as soon as I can, buddy." By then I felt the warm blood oozing down over the left side of my body. I reached under with my right hand to that area. Sure enough, it was thick, red blood. A feeling of increasing weakness spread through me as my vision dimmed. "Hurry, Corpsman, I'm losing blood," I pleaded.

"I hear you, Mac. I'm almost through with this man. Hang on." By now my fatigues on the left side of my chest were saturated with blood. I could feel it oozing through them. My vision was rapidly dimming. I was sweating like crazy. "Hurry, Corpsman. I'm bleeding to death."

"I just finished this man, Jim. I'll be there in a jiffy. Hold on, I'm coming." And he was. He knelt at my left side and lifted up my pack to check the wound in my back. There was a pause interrupted by a soft whisper, "Oh, my God, Jim!" There was another pause, and the corpsman broke out in loud, hilarious laughter. He just kept on laughing and laughing while I was lying there, dying and dying. What's this guy's problem? I thought he was cracking up. Finally he was able to control himself and stop.

"You dumb-ass Marine," he quipped, "there's nothing wrong with you. They hit you in your pork and beans."

Much can be said about the state of mind when one is dying. Jim did receive the Purple Heart Medal for bona fide wounds incurred later in battle.

The Pioneer

For several years Dr. Jack Lauck, his wife, Mary Ann, my wife, Joyce, and I celebrated the anniversary of Iwo Jima D-Day by going out to dinner on February 19. Dr. Lauck is Colonel Lauck. He also served in the Korean War as the commander of an assault rifle company. He served with distinction in the Marine Corps for thirty years. He obtained his master's degree as well as his Ph.D. in business management while in the Corps. This additional schooling and his second career speak for his exceptional motivation and ability. After Colonel Lauck retired from the Corps, he and his family moved to Muncie, Indiana, where he was appointed a professor of business management at Ball State University.

At our foursome dinner in 1984, we discussed initiating a reunion of regional veterans of the Iwo Jima battle to be held on an annual basis. In 1985, the first of a series of such meetings materialized. They have endured and thrived through the years to this day. During the 1990 reunion I struck up a conversation with one attendee who related that he was a member of the Fifth Pioneer Battalion in the battle at Iwo Jima.

In continuing the conversation, I mentioned that the surviving remnant of our outfit marched to the West Beach on D+35, turned in all the live ammunition we had, and sat there waiting to board ship a few hours later for the return voyage to Hawaii. Later I heard the rumor that a few Japanese holdouts came down that beach from the north in a last gasp banzai attack as we sat there disarmed, for all practical purposes. There had also been a Pioneer Battalion somewhere to our right. It, too, had been disarmed except for one man with a machine gun. He stopped that banzai single-handedly! I asked the Pioneer from the Fifth whether he had heard that story.

"No," he replied. "I've never heard anyone repeat that story to me. But I will say, I was the man with the machine gun! I wasn't about to part with it or its ammunition until we were safely aboard the ship." As it turned out, that enlisted man had more battle savvy than the command that had put out the order to turn in all of our ammo. Without that one man establishing security for all of us, we might have been helplessly slaughtered there on the West Beach. Of course, he never received any citation for bravery or meritorious duty, but he certainly should have.

Amazing Grace

He was brought into our aid station on a litter in the early days of battle. The litter was placed on the ground; the man was unconscious. His respirations were normal. His pulse was regular and of normal rate, and his blood pressure was 70mm systolic. A unit of plasma was started. We noted a small entry bullet wound precisely marking the midline of his brow at a level one and one-fourth inches above the very top of his nose. In the midline of the scalp of the opposite side of his head was another larger, irregular midline exit wound. Blood oozed from it slowly and meagerly. I remarked to a corpsman that the man's outlook was very bleak. We cleaned and dressed the wound of his brow, and the hair was then shaved from the exit wound of the occipital scalp. A dressing was applied at that site, and we completed his red tag. Jones recorded pertinent data in the aid station ledger, and the unconscious man was sent to the beach to be further evacuated to a ship. Nothing more was heard of that casualty. I presumed that he was on the KIA (Killed In Action) list.

Three months later his buddy came to the Second Battalion Sick Bay at Camp Tarawa, asked for me, and brought good tidings. He began by announcing receipt of a letter from the man who was written off as dead. He had been evacuated from the battle zone by ship after leaving Iwo Jima and was admitted several days later to a U.S. Naval hospital at Treasure Island, California. Two weeks later he regained consciousness but was totally blind. Two months later he regained intact, normal vision. He was whole once more and free of impairment!

That bullet must have passed brow to occiput, exactly between the great lobes of the brain, the right and left cerebral lobes, without directly damaging any brain tissue. His entire clinical picture as we saw it may have been caused by secondary swelling of brain tissue or by hemorrhage. Whichever it was, it caused pressure, which perhaps resulted in unconsciousness and shock. The bullet must have taken a path just above the optic nerves and caused secondary, mild, transient dysfunction due to swelling or hemorrhage. Pressure on those nerves resulted in temporary blindness, which cleared when the cause resolved.

To this day I still marvel at the man's recovery. It is illustrative that the difference between life and death in battle is sometimes measured in split seconds and/or millimeters.

Adolph Fang

Adolph was a sturdy, husky young Marine who was a member of the assault squad of his platoon in Fox Company. His weapon was the bazooka, an unconventional weapon in appearance and so named because of its resemblance to the bizarre instrumental contrivance of comedian Bob Burns of movie and radio fame (in that day). Fang's weapon also looked much like an oversize green bassoon. As a weapon, the bazooka was used at close-in positions to fire single rockets into enemy installations such as bunkers. Usually the bazooka man carried the weapon on his right shoulder as he moved into position to sight in on his target. His assistant, or loader, carried a canvas sack of rockets . He loaded the rocket near the rear end of the weapon as requested. As the command to fire was called back, the assistant triggered the electronic firing mechanism that propelled the rocket toward the target in the sights.

Fang's assistant was killed by enemy fire shortly after they hit the beach. Sergeant O'Keefe volunteered as assistant to replace the original. The rockets for the weapon were loaded with very high explosive and wreaked great havoc on targets they struck. One rocket could knock out a whole nest of machine guns when they were closely clustered. When fired as a direct hit through the narrow aperture of a bunker, the rocket usually killed all within and blew the concrete structure into pieces. In addition to these two men, another vital part of the assault squad was the man who carried the flame thrower tank in a backpack strapped over his shoulders like a knapsack and filled with the fiery fuel napalm. It was his job to mop up with the fiery napalm after the bazooka blew everything apart. Two riflemen completed the complement of the assault squad. It was their duty to provide protective fire for the bazooka man and also the flame thrower operator. Sergeant O'Keefe was in charge of this particular assault squad.

On D+5, the First Platoon waited and waited all afternoon for the order to move out and knock out a bunker just ahead. It was so well camouflaged that it was hard to spot. It held up the advance of Fox Company in line with flanking units. As soon as it was spotted, the order came. At last they would get their opportunity to destroy the bunker. Dusk was but a short time away. The assault squad moved out of its foxholes and on toward the stubborn target. Fang was in front with the bazooka, and O'Keefe was close behind. What they did not know was a second and silent and unrecognized machine gun was nearby. The moment they started forward, it opened fire. Fang took four slugs in his chest and one in his right shoulder. Mike Ladich and Billy Menges, the two riflemen, ran forward to help Fang. So did Russ Stephens, the flame-thrower man. Machine-gun fire was so intense they could not drag Fang backward to the company area. They took him forward a short distance to a large boulder or ledge where he was safe. Paul Bradford, one of the platoon corpsmen, came up to attend Fang.

Tanks were called forward to knock out enemy positions, and they did. His comrades loaded Fang on the front deck of one of the tanks, and he was hauled back to the aid station. He was on a litter when he arrived. It was lifted on to rock piles, which supported its ends about three feet above the ground. The wound in the shoulder was sprinkled with sulfa and dressed. Two of the chest wounds were sizable enough to permit air to be sucked through his chest wall. Sufficient air could collapse the entire lung. These holes were quickly sprinkled with sulfa, sutured, and dressed with thick battle dressings. A corpsman started plasma as we worked on the wounds. He was sent on back aboard the tank to a hospital.

Years later Fang told me it was dark when he arrived at the aid station. We had no lights because we were in the open. He also told me several Japanese officers were running around in the aid station swinging their swords. Even yet I can clearly see him lying there on the litter, asking whether he would qualify for a Purple Heart Medal. In my opinion, the degree of his shock plus the morphine were enough to sharply dim his vision. Concomitantly he had hallucinations about enemy soldiers running about swinging samurai swords. His wounds were obvious to me, as were the in-

111

struments and dressings. We were not disturbed by enemies and swords.

At the 1985 reunion on Long Island, Adolph Fang came at me from nowhere. He extended his hand as he exclaimed, "Dr. Brown, I want to shake your hand and thank you for saving my life on Iwo Jima forty years ago!"

Standing behind him, staring over the once-wounded right shoulder and dolefully shaking his head, was one of Fang's old-time Marine buddies, Mike Ladich. With a woeful expression on his face and with the same old GI wit as of yore, he commented, "You shouldn't have done it, Doc."

8

Burns

According to the Rules

In the course of the battle, four of the enemy were brought to our aid station for medical care. Three of them had suffered burns from flaming napalm or diesel oil. The burns were treated by applications of Vaseline gauze strips covered with thick battle dressings afterward. In turn, Ace bandages were wrapped snugly over the battle dressings to compress the wounds and to minimize loss of serum from the burned skin. The dressings were then secured with adhesive tape. These men were given morphine to relieve their pain, if needed. Later they were shipped back to the Fifth Division Station Hospital. Station hospitals were tent hospitals similar to those exhibited in the comedy series *M*A*S*H* on TV years later. The fourth enemy casualty we treated had a thigh badly torn by shrapnel. He was treated as we would have treated one of our own. Hemorrhage was stopped. The surrounding skin was cleansed with tincture of green soap. Sulfadiazine crystals were sprinkled over the open wound. Morphine was administered to relieve pain, and he was sent by ambulance to the division hospital.

Even though we hated their guts at that time, we were obliged to treat Japanese in a humane manner and did so. When the time came to us for disposition, the enemy were managed as fellow human beings, injured and needing help, not hatred. Their superiors promised the Japanese troops all kinds of barbaric cruelties should they fall into U.S. hands. Fear and apprehension were evident when they entered the aid station. These disappeared when they were offered cigarettes and food by our corpsmen. Some even smiled.

In prebattle training, we sometimes heard threats by Marines that if they ever captured a Japanese, they would kick him in the butt and gun him down as he ran away. Afterward I never heard any of them say they were a party to such an act or that they ever witnessed such acts. They were grim, fierce warriors, but those Marines on Iwo Jima had a soft spot for the wounded enemy. Some of those Marines may have been reluctant to admit having compassion, but they did.

Each assault squad included a flame-thrower man. These men were priority targets for snipers and machine gunners because they were obliged to stand or crouch while in action as they distributed fiery death and wounds. Tankers were better protected. The containers of napalm were targeted just as often as the carriers. Hitting the fuel tank wounded or destroyed the carrier as well as the tank. The portable tank was carried as a backpack in a harness of webbing, much like orchard- or lawn-spraying backpacks. The interior of the tank was pressurized in order to force the fuel out through a few feet of connecting hose to a tubular wand fitted with an electronic trigger and a nozzle. As the trigger released the flowing fuel out through the nozzle, a spark ignited it to throw forward for five or ten or maybe thirty feet the flaming jet.

As the jet was delivered into a cave or bunker opening, it burned occupants with its very hot liquid. It also consumed oxygen rapidly in enclosed spaces and caused suffocation. Flame-throwing tanks carried a cannonlike tube mounted on a rotary device that moved horizontally as well as vertically. The Napalm container of the flame-throwing tank was much, much larger than that of the infantryman's backpack. The treaded tanks could fire flaming streams as far as 150 feet. Napalm is highly flammable jellied gasoline, which produces tremendous heat when it burns and sears the skin deeply as it spatters.

On occasions when the flamethrowers' fuel supplies were exhausted and they were inconveniently far removed from replacement Napalm, our troops would pour two or three five-gallon tanks of diesel oil into the mouths of caves and ignite the oil by throwing a grenade in behind. The sparks from the exploding missile fired the oil. As the enemy fled in burning clothing from the caverns or emplacements, they were readily mowed down. Cruel? Yes. But what about war is not? Our task was to defeat the enemy that had bombed our nation in Pearl Harbor.

The Fiery Tank

Those roaring, dust-creating tanks with their heavy plates of steel always provided a sense of security when they roved by us, headed for some task up front. Up there they fired barrages from their small cannons and their heavy machine guns, and sometimes they hurled long tongues of fire from their huge flamethrowers. They imparted comfort to us and an air of invincibility as they rattled their grinding tractors on their way to hurl fear and havoc at the enemy troops. Those tanks would really let the enemy have it!

One day a small group of them hurtled invisibly by in a great cloud of dust and smoke a hundred and fifty yards away, trailing a tail of less dense dust a hundred yards long. How indomitable those tanks seemed. Suddenly a brief light appeared within that rolling cloud. It was followed by a huge fireball expanding upward and outward. Most of the tanks and the dust cloud moved on without hesitation, leaving behind one stationary vehicle.

From where we were, we could easily see the raging inferno as the tank's fuel and Napalm fed the smoking flames. It all subsided in a few minutes except for the glowing hot framework of the tank. Many of those thick steel plates simply melted away. In due time, as the skeletal remains cooled and blackened, tank officials came to inspect the lifeless catastrophe. Nothing was seen of the one-time occupants. The monster was mortal. No longer did it strike fear in the hearts of its successful destroyers, who had struck it down with a single artillery shell.

Loss of the tank was a stroke of ill fortune. Loss of its crew was horrifying and depressing, even though we may not have personally known the men in the crew caught in that instant ending of their lives in that hellish death trap. But we could very realistically conceive of ourselves fatefully exiting life in similar tragic, helpless circumstances. They didn't have a chance. We looked at the smoldering tank and wondered if a similar fate awaited us.

The Garbage Can

This is not meant to be facetious, but one member of our battalion was killed by a garbage can. Somewhere back of the cliffs, the enemy had a 402 mortar concealed in a cave. Occasionally the door of the cave that concealed it was opened and a launcher propelled out on several feet of tracks. The missile was too large to drop down the mortar tube, which might direct it more accurately. When the launcher reached the end of its track, a small missile was fired from behind it directly into the back end of the huge missile, which contained an explosive charge at its posterior end. This fired the huge shell, loaded with phosphorous, in an erratic trajectory toward Mount Suribachi at the south end of the island. Sometimes the shell went well out beyond the end. Sometimes it landed well north of Suribachi. Sometimes it veered to the right or left of a straight line. Two of these freaks landed in our battalion area.

As it was fired off the launcher and up through the air, the huge shell generated a weird sort of a *whoop, whoop, WHOOP* sound, which signaled its launching to everyone on the island. It must have been five or six feet long and fifteen inches or more in

116

diameter. Its velocity was slow, and its trajectory was low. Upon hearing the weird notification of such a flight, we looked upward, if unoccupied with casualties, and watched for it. It was readily visible as it cruised overhead. Other battalions had other names for it, but in our circles it was called *the Garbage Can,* a very appropriate name for the ballistic celebrity. Always as it approached above, someone shouted, "Here comes the Garbage Can!" In thirty seconds or so we sighted it wallowing through the air and on out into the ocean. Regarding the two that landed in or near our area, each at its concussion upon hitting the ground caused quite an explosion. Each burst into a huge fifty-foot-high fountain of fiery phosphorous particles like much-smaller Fourth of July fireworks. They were actually more rockets than mortars. One of those landed directly on an unfortunate member of our battalion, killing him immediately. All other ballistic missiles used in that battle were propelled with such speed that they were invisible in flight. Not being an ordnance expert, I cannot attest to the technical veracity of all the preceding description, but most of it is the truth as we saw it.

Unique Techniques

Most of our corpsmen were conscientious and serious with regard to their duties. Some exceeded their fulfillment of duty according to standards established by regulations. Bill Miller, for instance, designed a battle kit for corpsmen in which they stocked many more items than the GI type permitted. Bill's kit was much more efficient and practical. His design was approved by the regimental surgeon. He in turn submitted it to the surgeon of the Fifth Division. Twenty-one kits of Corpsman Miller's design were produced and distributed to corpsmen within our battalion. The men carrying them found them quite helpful, very much an improvement.

Two other corpsmen developed innovative techniques for managing phosphorous burns in ways rendering care more expeditiously at the front. Paul Bradford acquired butter from a member of the galley crew while he was still aboard ship and headed for Iwo, packed it in a metal container, and applied it immediately to those phosphorous burns he encountered at the front. The butter prevented the air from oxidizing the chunks of phosphorous and causing chemical burns. Dressings were then fixed in place over the damage.

Corpsman Glen Lougee noted the phosphorous particles were easily removed from the ulcers of burned skin by flipping the pieces out with the sharp point of his K-bar. That weapon is a sharp, oversized, hunting knife. He then applied Vaseline gauze and a battle dressing to such a wound. Removing the particles mechanically was logical. Healing began sooner.

The Michelin Man

He was cursing the enemy and the United States Marine Corps with equal vehemence as he was led into our aid station by a few of his fellowmen. A strong stench of phosphorous surrounded him. There were small black marks in the skin of his face and many more where chunks of the chemical had burned all the way through the front side of his green fatigue jacket. As I removed his jacket and cut away his green skivvy shirt to obtain a better view of the burns on his skin, he switched the direction of his fury, cursing even more venomously myself and the U.S. government. Exposure of the particles of phosphorous to the air and to perspiration caused faster and greater oxidation of the chemical and even greater, painful burning. He was really in tremendous, intense pain by this time as the result of multitudes of small, penetrating ulcers that peppered the skin of face, neck, chest, abdomen, thighs, and legs. In addition, he resented the disability for which we were treating him.

How did it happen? He was Platoon Sergeant Evans in Fox Company. He had carried a phosphorous grenade on each shoulder strap of his ammunition belt. As his squad moved forward toward an enemy position, a bullet struck one of the grenades and exploded it all over his front side. Literally hundreds of the tiny phosphorous bits burned through his clothing immediately and onto adjacent skin. There they created more havoc by burning even deeper. His platoon corpsman injected a syrette (half-grain) of morphine into one of his shoulders. The corpsmen in our aid station brushed off many particles with dry gauze or cotton. Washing with water or alcohol would have caused even more severe, deeper burns and more pain. Oily applications help phosphorous burns. We had an abundant quantity of Vaseline gauze intended for such use in our fifty-five-gallon steel drum of medical supplies. Grease coats the skin, the burns, and the phosphorous particles and thereby excludes the air from whatever it covers. We began applying three-by-eight-inch pieces of that impregnated gauze to his skin wherever burns were evident. After we applied the Vaseline gauze to a depth of three layers to all burned areas of the skin, we overlaid it with thick layers of battle dressings. Meanwhile we gave him a half-grain of morphine solution hypodermically. This afforded no relief, so I gave a grain of the analgesic by vein. This was a very large dose. It had about as much effect as did batting my eyelids.

The final step of the medical regime was to secure all those dressings to Evans's body. Rather than adhesive tape, I chose to use three-inch elastic Ace bandages, also in ample supply in the drum. The elastic bandage not only secured; it also compressed. This proves desirable and effective in inhibiting weeping of serum from the wounds. Losing serum means losing much fluid as well as vital chemical constituents in the fluid. Only the skin around his eyes, nostrils, and mouth were visible. Fortunately, the skin areas pertinent to his emunctories were uninvolved and required no cover.

When the masterpiece was complete, the suffering marine was still cursing away in undiminished volume. A chuckle started to bubble up within me. I repressed it rather than being offensive. He resembled very much the Michelin Man seen in so many auto tire advertisements prior to World War II. Evans was transported on back to the rear and directly to a ship that had good medical facilities for the wounded.

Seven years later at a reunion of the Fifth Marine Division Association in Chicago, a handsome, well-groomed young man nattily dressed in a sports jacket and slacks approached, shook my hand, and said, "Doctor, I wish to apologize to you."

"For what?"

"For cursing and damning you there in that aid station on Iwo Jima when you were doing everything possible to help me in those miserable circumstances." How overwhelming that moment was to me. Seven years later this unusual man, conscience-stricken by the offensive language he had used in that hour of excruciating pain, felt compelled to beg forgiveness. I was not at all offended then by his profanity. For him it was a sort of release at the time, a sort of reaction to his suffering. I understood. The wounds were more important to me. I paid little attention to the bad English.

"Say, Jack," I inquired, "what happened to you after we sent you back?"

"They transported me to a hospital ship. There the doctors read the notes you fellows made on my red tag. They let be that wonderful costume for two weeks. After removing what they conveniently could, they put me in a tub of warm water to soak away all the crusty stuff. After I was dry, they were unable to find a mark on me. My skin was completely healed!"

A bit of the scene came back to me then as I recalled working so diligently out there under the sky behind a measly pile of dirt and rocks, subjected to whining bullets and narrowly missing

120

shells. No, it wasn't state-of-the-art treatment, meticulously arranged and carefully supplied by a bevy of nurses in a sterile, air-conditioned surgery. But the results, thank God, could not have been better.

9

Shrapnel Wounds

Buddies: Green and Greene

One evening at about dusk Dog Company was involved in a skirmish up front. A small bevy of casualties suddenly flooded into our aid station. One of these was a Marine named Green. His buddy walked alongside the litter very attentively and continued his close observation as I knelt over the wounded, unconscious man on the litter. Green had a head wound caused by shrapnel from an artillery shell. Part of his skull was torn away; brain tissue hung and swelled through it. The normal convolutions and grooves were gone. This meant that substantial brain tissue had been destroyed. Moreover, he had an abnormal pattern of breathing. Just when I thought he had stopped breathing, the rapid cycle would start again.

That type of breathing was ominous. His buddy inquired as to my opinion of the situation. As an intern a little more than a year before, I had seen numerous instances of this abnormal Cheyne-Stokes pattern in stroke patients. It meant bad news and implied a bad prognosis. With all the brain damage and the abnormal type of breathing, it wasn't difficult to fathom that Green's viability was limited. I reported as much to his buddy. Moreover, I predicted that Green would die within two hours or so. His buddy asked whether he might stay with him.

"You certainly may," I replied, touched by his sincerity. "What's your name, anyway?"

"Greene."

"Brothers?" I asked, imagining the horror it must have been to see a brother in that fatal condition.

"No, I spell my name with three *e*s."

When the ambulance came, I allotted both spaces on it to casualties with a more hopeful outlook. Green survived three more hours under the watchful eyes of Greene. The next morning Greene went forward again to his company. He was killed in battle the afternoon of the same day.

Leon Justice: His Version

At the 1991 Fifth Marine Division Association Reunion in San Diego, Leon Justice swaggered toward me on crutches. His right trouser leg was neatly folded upward and pinned to his belt strap. He greeted me with the warmest of smiles and hailed me.

"Hey, Doc! I'm Leon Justice. You probably don't remember me." As if to better identify himself, he continued, "It was day seven on Iwo. We jumped off as usual at eight o'clock that morning. They saw us coming. It wasn't long until their artillery dropped in on us. One landed close to me. When the dust cleared and I regained my senses, I realized it caught me in the right thigh. Shrapnel sheared it off up pretty high. As I looked about, I spotted the lower half of my right leg with the foot still attached lying a few feet away. When some corpsman put me on a stretcher, I reached out for the leg and lay it across my abdomen. I read an article sometime before about doctors sewing severed legs or arms back on after accidents, and I just knew they could do the same for me. I clung desperately to my limb, unwilling to let go. There in the aid station I heard one of your corpsmen say, 'Dr. Brown, Leon Justice won't give me his foot and leg. What should I do?'

"You looked over at me and casually replied, 'Oh, just tie it to his good leg, and ship him on back.'"

We had a protocol, which in Leon's case would have been to dig a hole in the sand and bury the remnant leg. Poor Leon did not realize the impossibility of having his mangled extremity restored. He was still too stunned by the explosion to comprehend the gravity of the wound. He seemed much calmer when the leg stayed with him. He was shipped back and ultimately berthed in a hospital ship. The amazed doctors aboard dropped slanderous remarks about the kooks up front who bound useless parts to the wounded before transporting them to the rear. Forty-six years later, Leon took great delight in relating his story, and I as much in listening to it.

Leon Justice: Lougee's Version

Four years later at the fifty-year reunion in St. Louis, Ed Jones hurried toward me and began quite excitedly, "Glen Lougee is here! I just talked to him. I'd recognize him anywhere by his funny walk. We hadn't seen each other for fifty years, and I spotted him in that mob."

Together we searched for Lougee until we found him. That evening, Mr. and Mrs. Roy Brown, Mr. and Mrs. Tony Moreno, Glen Lougee, Joyce, and I had a wonderful dinner and evening together. In the course of many wonderful recollections the corpsmen and I shared with the wives, we made it eventually to the story of the rescue and treatment of Leon Justice. Lougee's story of the case was a bit different from Leon's. Lougee told us that Leon was an ex-Paratrooper who was in combat in the Solomon Islands. He learned to tell whether the enemy was approaching in combat by the sound level of its gunfire.

Glen Lougee told us the following story: "Leon Justice and I became good friends during the months of training which preceded combat. In a very serious conversation just prior to hitting Iwo, Leon said to me, 'Looj, if I ever get hit, don't leave me lying out there in No-Man's Land. Take me on back. Promise.'

"One morning we really got into it with the Japs. A runner from headquarters company informed me that Justice was sent forward fifty yards beyond the front lines to place air markers. We needed help. Mortar shells bombarded the area. Leon failed to return. Someone instructed me to go check on him. I left, going in the designated direction. The farther I advanced, the worse the mortar barrage became. It was no use to call out to him, so great was the din. Knowing he was out there and in trouble kept me searching.

"Five minutes later I stumbled into him and found him in a semistupor. A large, gaping, bloody stump terminated what was left of the right thigh. The heavy rain of mortar fire continued. We both needed cover. Justice was a large, husky fellow, too large for me to handle by myself. I was about to start back for help when a Marine, Gilman Horgan, came by. We dragged him, pain, hemorrhage, and all, across the ground to a low spot, which offered a bit of shelter. We asked the frightened occupants already there to make way so we might treat Justice in that low spot. One of them went back for litter bearers.

"I gave Leon a shot of morphine. We spread a poncho on the ground and slid Leon over on it, gripping the severed remnant of his thigh as best we could to stop blood loss. The other Marine was kneeling by Leon's right side, reaching down, and using a battle dressing to put pressure on the bleeding artery, as I instructed him to do. Meantime, kneeling by his left side, I mixed some plasma and started it in Leon's left arm. All at once, as I was still kneeling out on the left side, a mortar shell exploded loudly a few feet to Horgan's left. We both turned and looked. As I turned back, I stared into Horgan's eyes for just an instant. Then it happened. Another mortar shell exploded closer to Horgan. He disappeared, just like that. Everything went black for me. The force of the concussion numbed and blinded me. I could not move or think. I was certain I was dying. Blood oozed down across my face and on into my mouth.

"I felt a hard lump in my chest. Something was broken. I reached it with my right hand and, on touching it, realized it was my pistol tucked under my fatigue jacket. As I pulled my hand down and across my body, something sharp stuck out at my belt line. Automatically I reached up with the other hand and wiped my face. A tremendous light poured into my eyes. I wasn't blind after all, and I was still alive.

"Turning over, I rose to my knees. Leon was lying there clear out of it in a stupor. Pieces of meat were sticking to my uniform. It wasn't mine, nor was the blood which ran into my mouth. Leon started moaning. Part of Horgan's trunk, a section of his disintegrated body, lay across Leon's chest. I lifted my hands to remove it, and realized his entrails were lashed across my arms. Feces oozed from an open end of one of the pieces. A sharp piece of bone stuck outward from my belt. Very slowly it dawned on me that Horgan took a direct hit from the shell. The Marine came with the litter bearers and stretcher. They lifted Leon onto it and headed for the aid station. You were busy working on someone else. My right hip was hurting. Dr. Collins checked it and ordered another corpsman to care for my wounds. Whoever it was pulled pieces of shrapnel out of them, poured sulfa crystals into them, and taped on a thick dressing. After Leon was shipped out on an ambulance, I rested a bit longer until I was more settled. I put on my helmet, slung my medical kit over my shoulder, grabbed my rifle, and headed back up to our platoon."

Loss of our Leader

Maj. John W. Antonelli graduated from the U.S. Naval Academy at Annapolis. He requested duty with the U.S. Marine Corps, the amphibious arm of our Navy. He commanded a Raider battalion in the Solomon Island battles of the South Pacific, during the early part of the war in the Pacific. When the Fifth Marine Division was commissioned at Camp Pendleton in early 1944, he was placed in command of the Second Battalion, Twenty-seventh Marines. After a month or so of duty in that battalion, I was asked to report to his office. As I was not aware of involvement in any military miscreance, that order was a matter of concern to me.

The meeting was brief. The major addressed me tersely: "Doc, you're a Marine now. At future social gatherings of this battalion or of our regiment, you will be expected to wear Marine Corps officers' attire and insignias. Get rid of those Navy blues."

That hurt. Two months before, I had spent all of my officer's uniform allowance of $400 on those blues, whites, and a greatcoat. Now, $200 more, this time out of my own pocket, was much more than a month's pay. The new uniform would break me financially, and our marriage was but three weeks away. What a low blow.

"Yes, sir." That and no more was spoken in all due obeisance. It was followed by one big, fat salute. Turning about, I walked from his office.

The major was a stocky, vigorous, plain-spoken, no-nonsense man. He was somewhat rotund at the equator. Little did I surmise that he was one of the best. Troops of his command sang a little doggerel titled "Antonelli and His Belly." He feigned ignorance of the ditty, but we knew better. He was beloved by his men and highly respected. A tender heart lay under his gruff exterior. When a corpsman returned from over the hill after spending most of the week AWOL to see his wife and their newborn babe, the major gave him a few days of brig time and told us to "bust" him one grade. He immediately told us to restore the grade in thirty days because the corpsman had one more mouth to feed and would need more money. He also recommended we advance the corpsman another rate as soon as feasible.

In late November 1944, Dr. Collins received orders to immunize every man in the battalion with one-half cc of yellow fever vaccine. At the designated hour, all battalion personnel walked two by two through our Sick Bay to receive the "shot" in the bulky shoulder muscle (deltoid) of one arm or the other. In those days all syringes were made of glass. For this session we used sterile 10 cc syringes filled to the top mark with a vial of the vaccine, a quantum of the dry powder to which we added 19 cc sterile water. A sterile needle was replaced after being used in the administration of twenty immunizations.

Twenty minutes after the entire battalion was immunized, Chief Ph M Milt Klinger sought me at the Sick Bay to inform me that one of the corpsmen gave Major Antonelli the entire syringe full in one injection. What a shocker that was. It aroused much trepidation. A court-martial trial and dishonorable discharge certainly awaited me should the major suffer a significant complication from the overdose.

I inquired, "Milt, do you have any knowledge of our commander's current status?"

"Yes, I do, Dr. Brown. I just passed him in the Camp Street as I came here."

"OK, Milt. We will both keep our mouths tightly buttoned on this matter and keep watch for any undesirable reaction."

None occurred, and after two weeks I was at ease. Major Antonelli was never informed of the overdose. I never understood why everyone was immunized with that vaccine, unless it was anticipated that we would relocate in some area where the disease was endemic.

In the midportion of the battle the enemy became quite resistant to the efforts of the Twenty-seventh. Major Antonelli and Col. Dan Duryea, who had command of the First Battalion four days earlier when Colonel Butler was killed, were designated to lead their units in a jump-off assault against the enemy. Each commander, along with his runner, or aide, drove from his respective CP, then walked to an advanced position beyond the front lines in order to attract less attention, as well as to gain a better view of the terrain beyond, where the enemy waited. From that vantage point, the commanders searched for evidence of enemy installations ahead and made their advance tactical decisions.

As the two officers walked back to their vehicles, Colonel Duryea called to his aide, who hastily rushed toward him. As he neared, he stepped on a very powerful antipersonnel mine. The aide was killed. One piece of shrapnel severed the officer's right forearm just below the elbow. Another partially severed his left knee. Major Antonelli was standing in a position more remote from the explosion. Much sand and other debris was blown against his face and neck. He was blinded by all the foreign material blown into his eyes from the ground before him.

When he was borne into the aid station on a litter, Major Antonelli's facial skin was marked by many tiny bleeding scratches caused by the blasted particles of sand and rocky grit. It was red and swollen. So were his eyelids. The sclerae (whites of the eyes) were fiery red and puffy. He could see light but no figures of men or objects.

We irrigated Major Antonelli's eyes with normal saline solution and instilled an analgesic eye ointment in them. His eyes were next covered by patches. We secured them with roller bandage wrapped about his head. Adhesive tape would have caused untold pain were it sealed to the bleeding, swollen skin of his face. He was transported to the division hospital. From there he went to a hospital ship or a ship with adequate equipment for management of his eyes and stayed there until near the end of the conflict. He maintained communication with his replacement in command, Maj. Jerry Russell.

As we sat on the west beach of Iwo Jima waiting to board ship the afternoon of March 26, we were cheered by a surprise visit by Major Antonelli. He wore dark sunglasses for the sake of his eyes. One side of his face was still marred by scratches and bruises. He walked among his men, cheering, encouraging, and thanking them for serving so well. His presence gave us all a lift of spirits. The next morning he boarded a plane to fly back to Hawaii and on to Camp Tarawa, where he began preparing for our return and planning for training for the next operation, the assault on Japan.

In the spring of 1999, Brig. Gen. John W. Antonelli died of natural causes. Great was the admiration with which we spoke of him at the annual meeting of the Fifth Marine Division Association at Albuquerque the following July. We were all proud to have served under such a distinguished, capable leader.

Irony

On an afternoon when Dog Company was exchanging amenities in a very fierce firefight with the enemy, one of its riflemen was seriously wounded in the abdomen by a bullet. His wound was treated immediately and appropriately by the platoon corpsman. Meanwhile, four litter bearers appeared on the scene, bearing a litter for the wounded rifleman. He was transferred to the litter from the ground on which he lay and was soon on his way back to the rear, an area with slightly more safety. Suddenly out of nowhere a grenade came rolling across the ground and stopped just under the litter. As one of the litter bearers stooped to throw the grenade out of harm's way, it exploded with great force, killing the litter bearer and, as fate would have it, the wounded man on the litter.

Orders Are Orders

Early in the afternoon of the third day of battle I was called to the nearby CP by Major Antonelli. He took me forward several yards, pointed farther forward and a little to the right, and instructed me, "See those trees over there? Lieutenant Fitch and his platoon are in reserve there. Antipersonnel shells hit the branches of those trees. The shrapnel that showered below badly wounded Fitch and his corporal. You take some corpsmen and litters and go take care of them."

"Yes, sir." "Those trees" to which the Major referred were actually scrubby vegetation that had already been shell-shocked several times. Between us and the trees were three hundred yards of bare ground, which appeared to be as level as a pool table and just as barren. I didn't want to make that trip. We would be visible all over the place from Mount Suribachi at the rear and the cliffs up front and to all the snipers and bunkers in between. But one does not negotiate such orders. Taking a very deep breath, I headed back to our battalion aid station, knowing full well we would never make it unscathed.

Hastily grabbing my medical kit and slinging it over my left shoulder, I turned and issued orders to four corpsmen to accompany me across the bare area. The trip across the clear, flat, barren stretch of battlefield was surprisingly uneventful. I must have overestimated the situation. On arriving at the destination we found Lt. Fitch to have a sucking hole in his chest wall caused by shrapnel. His corporal had a large, irregular linear open wound in his abdominal wall. I ordered a corpsman to sprinkle sulfadiazine crystals in the wound and to close the walls of the wound with long strips of adhesive tape. While I was sewing closed the hole in the lieutenant's chest, two other corpsmen were starting plasma in the casualties and the fourth was administering a syrette of morphine to each. In ten minutes we were ready to start the return trip. The wounded were placed on litters; four Marines jumped out of their foxholes to help the corpsmen carry the litters, and away we went on the return trip. I was walking between the two litters and their bearers when the fun began.

As we completed the first fifty yards of the journey, an enemy's small mortar shell burst a short distance behind the second litter. One of the Marines was hit in the leg by a piece of shrapnel and dropped out. A replacement jumped out of his foxhole and took over. We didn't miss a step. But those devils had been watching us all the time from their hiding places. They had waited until we were moving more slowly with our burdens on the way back to begin firing at us. After exhorting the first litter bearers to hurry, I turned and beckoned the second group to come faster. Hurrying in the loose, sandy soil was almost impossible. We were encouraged by more mortar shells, which seemed to be tracking us every thirty seconds at a distance some thirty feet immediately behind us.

We made it back to our shell-hole aid station and immediately transported Fitch and his corporal on back to the rear on our ambulance. Both survived. We didn't have much time to relax, though, for another casualty was soon brought in. As I opened my medical kit, I was surprised to see a disc-shaped piece of shrapnel edged up to the back side of the kit. It had penetrated glass vials, a roll of tape, some roller gauze, and two battle dressings before coming to a rest against the canvas wall of the kit. It was an inch and a half in diameter. Its center was a half-inch thick, and it tapered to the periphery as a discus does. Had it not been for the medical kit, that bit of shrapnel would have torn into my hip and disabled me for months or even longer.

An Unpretentious Hero

None of the corpsmen of Fox Company were killed at Iwo Jima. Despite their daring escapades, their selflessness in the face of danger, and the terrible wounds suffered by some of them, all survived. They had their lives on the line just as often as corpsmen of the other rifle companies in our battalion. It is my very firm belief each one of that group possessed feline survival genes similar to those of tomcats.

Ph M 2/C Fred Alberty was one of that group of corpsmen. He came into our battalion early in its existence. A bit of a loner, in the field he did his share. He had fun with others both in camp and on liberty. When I first met him he was wearing a gold-colored earring. Having never seen young men of his age in Indianapolis or Detroit wearing earrings, I presumed him to be some sort of street rowdy from Los Angeles.

During one torrid firefight in which many troops were injured or killed, one of the Fox Company Marines was badly injured by shrapnel, Alberty attended him, and when he was finished he and two Marines transferred the wounded man to a litter. Along with another Marine and Alberty, they started carrying the wounded Marine to the rear. They had gone but a few yards when a barrage of mortar shells began pouring into the area. The three Marines quickly dropped the litter and jumped into nearby foxholes. Alberty gently, quickly, lowered to the ground the litter handle he was holding. He crouched over the wounded Marine, protecting him from further injury with his own body, and stayed in that position for several minutes, until the barrage ended. For this heroic act especially, he was awarded the U.S. Navy Silver Star Medal. Fred Alberty was for real.

Gotcha!

Our aid station was lambasted frequently and without respite for as long as fifteen to twenty minutes at a time. Ten of our rifle company corpsmen were killed or wounded and evacuated on the first day. We could ill afford the loss of any of our two-doctor, seven-corpsman group. One of them, Jim White, was a full-blooded hillbilly from the mountains of eastern Tennessee. He had spent three years in the Civilian Conservation Corps before enlisting in the Navy. Another corpsman, Junior Funk, had signed up immediately after graduating from high school in Corvallis, Oregon. They were alike as apples and onions, but they were bosom buddies. War creates unanticipated friendships. They were an unusual pair.

133

Their foxholes on that particular day were about fifteen feet from mine and were separated from each other by a wall of earth eighteen inches wide. We occupied foxholes located alongside the north bank of Airfield #1 when the bombardment started. It began with occasional explosions. The Japs were probably sighting in on us. Soon the bombardment intensified with each passing moment. One of those two corpsmen was standing in his own foxhole. White, the taller, was kneeling in his. Only their helmeted heads were visible as they chatted across the dividing wall. Their conversation was inconsiderately interrupted by a bursting mortar shell, which landed in the very middle of the barrier separating their shelters. There went two of our corpsmen. *How will we manage?* I wondered. As the dust and smoke cleared, the very crests of the two helmets rose ever so slowly at the surfaces of their foxholes and edged on upward in minute increments.

Imagine their amazement as those two pairs of eyes met just above ground level, each man certain that his buddy had been killed! Their joy was shared by me as I sighed in relief. I was certain the two of them were dead. But no, that soft, loose soil had absorbed the violence of the exploding shell, including its concussion. The pieces of cruel flying shrapnel were stopped in the beginning of flight by that interval of ground. The moments between the explosion and the initial appearance of the gradually rising helmets lasted seemingly so long. What breathholding moments those were. Great relief was shared by all of our little but much-needed band.

The Metallic Marine

On February 25, 1945, Lt. Tilghman's First Platoon of Fox Company was moving through Death Valley in a push against the enemy. A red-hot firefight was under way. Nineteen-year-old Ed Perry stopped at the edge of a deep shell hole to gain protection within it. Sergeant Pietrowski called to him to keep moving, warning that the Japanese had already zeroed in on it. Ed walked about twenty-five more paces forward and a large shell exploded behind him. He felt a large piece of shrapnel rip into his lower back area. The force of the explosion blew him up and around through the air like a leaf blowing about in the wind. While he was whirling around, he felt something tear into his shoulder. He thought it was machine-gun bullets.

When he came down he landed on his back and rolled over. As he did so he was unable to move his left hand and forearm. He looked over at the left shoulder and saw nothing but raw meat and blood where his shoulder had been. Again he tried moving the left upper extremity. It was powerless. Another Marine walked over to him, unscrewed the cap of his canteen, and put it on the ground where Ed could reach it with his right hand, encouraging him that he would be OK. Shortly afterward, Corpsman Bradford was bending over Ed. Bradford poured sulfadiazine crystals into the shoulder wound, applied a dressing, and shot him with a morphine syrette. Bradford then turned him onto his left side and observed a strip of flesh, torn partly from his lower back and partly from the upper hip, but still fixed at one end. He pushed the chunk of flesh back in place, sprinkled it with sulfa, and bandaged it tightly as he taped it securely to both sides of Ed's trunk. Bradford said the lower end of the spinal column was exposed.

Some of his comrades slid Ed onto a poncho and carried him down to the beach. He was short, stocky, and heavy. They left him at a first-aid station on the beach. Intravenous plasma was started in his right arm. He saw many other wounded men on litters at the aid station. They were attended by corpsmen and doctors. From there he was transported to a hospital ship, which sailed on down to Saipan. All hospital beds at Saipan were filled. The ship sailed on to Guam. All U.S. Navy hospital beds there were likewise filled. Ed was admitted to an Army hospital where he underwent two minor surgeries for removal of debris from his wounds.

From Guam, Ed was shipped to Pearl Harbor and the Aiea Heights Naval Hospital. From there, he was moved to Oak Knoll Navy Hospital at Oakland, California. Two months later he was transported to the Naval Hospital at Oceanside, where he underwent therapy for rehabilitation. Two months later he was released home on convalescent leave. A few weeks later one of his wounds started draining. He was admitted to a Navy hospital in Philadelphia for treatment. There he was told he had about forty pieces of shrapnel in the back of his chest and approximately one hundred small pieces in the low back area. After all those hospitalizations, he was reasonably intact. Today motion is still limited in the left shoulder. Whenever he passes through airport security scanners, he still sets them off and requires special disposition. Once his convalescence was complete, he was able to enter college, where he pursued a degree in business administration. After graduation he found work in a bank and eventually became its executive vice president and loan officer. He married the light of his life, a nurse whom he had met while in college. With a family of three children they lived very, very happily until her demise after fifty-four years of marriage.

Valley of the Shadow

Easy Company was on a push through Death Valley. Someone had decided to jump off in assault in the late afternoon and surprise the enemy. It all began without the usual preliminary shelling. The going was rough and through rocky, uneven ground near the edge of the West Beach. Several small bushes dotted the view ahead and made spotting anything significant difficult. The advance was resisted to a standstill by a large Nambu machine gun, probably in an undetected pillbox. Rifleman Leonard Nederveld finally spotted it and was about to fire a clip of bullets through the aperture when his sergeant ordered him not to fire. He told Leonard to swing around to the side, sneak up on it, and throw a grenade at it. He hit a bull's-eye, as the grenade went right through the port opening. It detonated within and set off a horrendous series of explosions out of all proportion to what ordinarily occurred in those circumstances. Everyone was startled. Bullets and other missiles flew wildly through the air at nothing in particular. Later it was determined that the pillbox was an ammunition depot stocked full of various sorts of deadly weapons and missiles. Leonard told me they found a tunnel connecting that pillbox to another, also similarly stocked, and the whole system went up in the myriad explosions.

Some Marines were injured as a result. Nederveld was not to be found. He was most certainly killed in the mammoth explosion. Night soon came and all was quiet. About twenty-four hours later an unidentified figure was spotted wiggling and snaking along the ground on his front side, inching along very slowly toward the U.S. lines. Obviously it was one of the enemy attempting to sneak through the area to commit some kind of mayhem. One of the Marines raised his rifle to shoot the figure. Someone yelled, "Don't shoot. It's a Marine!"

Two men ran out in front to rescue him. The injured man was not recognizable. Rebstock thought he was Watson. The other rescuer insisted he was Nederveld. Whoever, he was thickly covered with dust and carbon from the explosion and with dirt. Dried blood encircled his mouth.The skin of his face was puffy and swollen and covered with fine, bleeding scratches and little black dots of shrapnel. His eyelids were swollen. The whites of the eyes were bloodred and congested. He was placed on a poncho, and some of his fellow Marines began a trip back to the aid station with their cargo. Mortar shells dropped and exploded around them. They dumped the wounded man in a shell hole and jumped in after him. Rebstock said later it was a wonder Nederveld wasn't killed by all those piling in over him.

Nederveld still does not recall anything about the explosion.

When he awakened, he was greeted by bright daylight. As he looked about, he estimated the enemy line was about 150 yards beyond where he lay. His platoon area seemed to be about fifty feet in the other direction. He wasn't sure. He feared if he moved, the enemy would spot him and shoot. He lay still for a long time. Everything was quiet. He decided to go for it and slid along on his belly, pulling himself along with a crooked left arm, then reaching forward with the right. He repeated this maneuver over and over, slowly progressing back to his own unit. He looked up and saw someone pointing a rifle in his direction. He screamed, "Don't shoot!" His voice was so weak, he didn't think anyone heard him. Two Marines ran out toward him, picked him up, and carried him on back. Someone started working on his sore places. His vision was dim, and he couldn't see who it was. They placed him on a stretcher and started to carry him back. All at once they threw him in a hole. He blacked out again and later awakened in a military hospital.

A Corpsman and His Can of Corn

Jerry Cunningham was as fond of canned whole-kernel corn as I was fond of tinned salted peanuts. His mother sent him a small supply from time to time. When we shipped out for battle, he stuck a can or two in his top knapsack to supplement K-Rations while in battle. My peanuts were squirreled away in my lower pack. That lower pack was sent ashore late on D-Day and stashed with everyone else's in a knapsack dump next to our ammo dump. When the Japanese spotted our ammunition stores on Iwo, they made the pile a prime target. Unfortunately, when the ammo dump was blown up so was the dump of lower packs located nearby. Personally, I think they targeted my peanuts.

The evening before he was wounded, Jerry treated himself to a dessert, his last can of whole-kernel corn. Early the following morning Fox Company jumped off into a red-hot firefight. Corpsman Cunningham was up front running about caring for the wounded. As he knelt over one of the Marines, Cunningham saw a grenade roll across the ground and directly under his abdomen. It exploded so rapidly, he never had a chance to throw it back. A piece of shrapnel slit his abdomen, and as he rose to his knees a loop of glistening bowel slid out through the wound. He had the presence of mind to attempt to shove it back into the abdominal cavity. The more he stuffed it, the more the bowel slithered through the slit. Suddenly a gash in the exposed bowel opened and undigested whole-kernel corn spewed out onto the ground. At that moment Bill Miller ran to Cunningham's aid, applying two large battle dressings over the exposed bowel. Miller then called to some litter bearers to take Jerry to our aid station.

Jerry stated that Dr. Collins examined him and told corpsmen what to do for him. Klinger was leaving just as Jerry was brought in. When Klinger returned, the corpsmen had not yet completely cared for Jerry, who was still lying on the litter. Becoming a bit irate at the slow pace of activity, Klinger commandeered an ambulance to take Cunningham to better facilities. As they carried him out of the aid station, Jerry winked at me and commented, "Doctor, I don't think I shall ever eat whole-kernel corn again! It doesn't digest very readily in me." The complications in his abdomen and damage to other parts caused eight months of hospitalization, surgeries, and rehabilitation to restore him to normal.

My Own Wounds

Late in the afternoon of D+23 the Second Battalion CP moved forward about four hundred yards and our aid station did likewise. We selected for our location a site that was a marked vertical indentation in a cliff about ten feet high. Our area was enclosed by the semicircular cliff wall. For all intents and purposes it was a good, well-protected spot for the aid station. Shortly after we arrived, three of us were standing about five feet forward from the back side of the shelter on a low shelflike elevation of ground. The mouth of a cave was but a few feet to our right. As we casually shot the breeze, I heard a brief hiss above my head, followed immediately by a loud shellburst when the mortar missile struck the wall directly behind us.

One of the other two men was knocked to the ground. The concussion seemed to give me a hard shove, which propelled me forward. A sharp, small pain appeared in the low back area. Dr. Tom Collins checked the small skin wound in the midline of the low lumbar area and found nothing more. My combat jacket was sprayed with so much fine shrapnel that it appeared to have been invaded by a small army of moths. A few little shrapnel holes were also present in the backs of my combat boots. They evacuated me to the Fifth Division hospital. The doctors there were very busy operating on wounded men whose injuries were far more serious than mine. Another ambulatory casualty and I were instructed to have a seat on the ground of a tent serving as an anteroom of some sort. We chatted a bit and in an hour or so fell asleep At dawn the next morning I donned my pack and helmet, slung my carbine over my shoulder, and headed up forward to our aid station. Constant activity marked that facility, allowing no time for being morbid or worrying about one's self.

A nagging, jabbing pain seemed to stick the midline of the lower portion of my back every time I bent over or rotated the trunk to either side. Eight days later, because the pain persisted, I wandered over to Dr. Hely's Third Battalion Aid Station. After listening to my sad story, he ordered me to pull up my skivvy shirt and to bend forward. About thirty seconds later he proclaimed "OK, mate, here it is." In the jaws of a hemostat he was holding a sliver of shrapnel about three-fourths of an inch long and one-eighth-inch in diameter. It wasn't very large, but it sure was an ornery little dickens. One end had been sticking the spinous process of one of the lower lumbar vertebrae. Some of my wise-acre children used to accuse me of running from the enemy.

In 1990, when my left knee was x-rayed prior to unrelated surgery, a small, radio-opaque, irregular metal foreign body was noted deep in the midportion of the thick, left gastrocnemius muscle (calf muscle) below. By this time it was a little rusty.

MIA to KIA

Corpsman Paul Bradford related, "On March fourth, D-plus-thirteen, we hit the deck as an artillery barrage began bombarding our area. Shrapnel from two different shellbursts hit me. Sergeant Moffat was lying on the ground not far from me. One of the two shells landed directly on him. We never did find his body afterward.

"The shrapnel injury was very painful. After action quieted a bit, I went back to our aid station, where someone checked the wounds and dressed them. I hung around the aid station a couple days and helped care for incoming casualties. By that time I improved considerably. I went back up to Fox Company.

"After we returned to Camp Tarawa, Carl Schraiber, the other corpsman in our platoon, and I were requested to depose affidavits regarding Sergeant Moffat's demise and destruction by the shell which struck him. The affidavit provided the information necessary to change his military status from Missing In Action to Killed In Action."

Death of a Hero

A misty daylight had enveloped us for more than an hour. Drifting toward us were odors of sulfurous fumes in steam vented up through volcanic rock formations from somewhere deep, deep below. Chilly morning breezes blew in over the nearby west coast-line. We who manned the Second Battle Aid Station ended our brief morning social hour by washing our hands and faces in a quart of water warmed in our individual helmets by two ignited heat tablets. After spending half of the previous night standing or sitting watch in a foxhole, those not already alert were rendered so by the crack of a sniper's rifle and the instantaneous hiss of a passing bullet.

Items used in the morning readiness—the bar of hard-water soap, toothpaste, toothbrushes, razors, combs, and shaving cream (if we even shaved)—were stashed back in our green ditty bags and the drawstring pulled snug at the free end. The ditty bags were in turn stashed away in our nearby backpacks for another twenty-four hours. We next arranged aid station gear in readiness for the fruit of battle action, as we knew it. Small and large battle dressings made by volunteer groups of women back home were placed conveniently. Adhesive tape, Band-Aids, merthiolate, alcohol, packets of sulfadiazine crystals, morphine syrettes, units of plasma and of serum albumin, our few surgical instruments, folded litters, and patient restraints were placed in proper order should they be needed for the care of wounded men evacuated from a firefight at the front just ahead of us.

We were ready and waiting, chatting about nothing in particular. Someone mentioned a Saturday night spent in an old fleabag hotel in LA—anything to get away from the military routine while on liberty. Another remembered the time Baron Hoffman threw a grenade in the only commode, a community affair, at one end of the fifth floor of the Hayward. Another read a letter from a former schoolmate now at the front with the AUS in France. And another one from a kid brother in western Illinois telling of his first quail hunt. The subjects were endless and seemed so disconnected from the real life of our aid station where the roof was the sky and the floor the natural soil of decayed volcanic rocks. Bits of walls were a few small, irregular piles of dirt and scattered collections of craggy volcanic stones, relics of eruptions of the remote past. A few peripheral foxholes were dug in the ground off to the right. In these we had spent the previous three nights. Our dirty green uniforms had been worn constantly ever since we came ashore. The only aspect of them not grimy was the black USMC insignia stamped on the flap topping the left pockets of our blouses. None of us wore the Red Cross armband, for we were told during training that the Japanese snipers loved to use those for target practice. Despite all the dirt, inconvenience, and less-than-gourmet breakfasts, we were ready for the day ahead, come what may.

The hour was 0730; the day, March 8, 1945. Those at home halfway around the world were just going to bed or were well into the night's sleep. The night before, the Fifth Marine Division headquarters sent orders to its Twenty-seventh Regiment command to breach that impenetrable wall of resistance with which the enemy troops had stopped our advance for two days. The message was hurried down to our Second Battalion. Major Antonelli called his company commanders into conference in a low, dimly lighted tent to discuss the push. Easy Company was to lead. Lt. Jack Lummus, one of the few remaining officers in that company, was appointed to direct the attack. Jack was a leader, not a director. As a Raider under the command of Major Antonelli, Jack had fought in South Pacific island battles.

Jack was a tall, tough, lean, wiry Texan reared near Ennis. To me, his features were those of a classic cowpoke. He was mild-mannered and very strong and had a soft, slow way of speaking in a Texas drawl. He wasn't much of a talker, yet he was quite sociable. He also had a unique way of talking and grinning at the same tine. In his college days he had played football at Baylor University, where he had been an All-American selection. At Camp Tarawa, I watched him run a few times; with his long stride his lean body seemed to glide along a foot above the ground, as the swift gazelle does. Major Antonelli was quite fond of Jack, but no more so than the men who had served under him in previous battles. He kept a picture of a very lovely young lady on his side of a table that he shared with four other officers in their tent at camp.

Back in our aid station, our knowledge of action was based on reports of the wounded we attended and from those who had assisted them back to us. We heard a few rumors about an all-out assault that morning. Someone told us the Twenty-seventh Regimental command had requested three tanks to lead the way. Being ignorant of the master plan for the day, we waited, hoping for the best, preparing for the worst. That fixed front was a deadly area. When three tanks rumbled by seventy yards to our right, we appreciated the accuracy of the scuttlebutt. As their cannons and machine guns blazed away, we knew the assault was under way. When the tanks moved on forward beyond our troops, Lummus and his men jumped out of their foxholes and followed along, firing with everything they had. They were ready to go. Some of the men who survived that assault told me later that as Lummus rushed forward he ran about pounding on the tanks with the butt of his carbine to get the attention of the gunners inside so he could yell to them the positions of targets at which they must fire. He ran wildly about without concern for his own safety, bravely shouting orders, throwing rocks at anyone he thought was shirking, and always moving forward. They breached the stonewall enemy line, running on and on, many passing Lummus as the charge accelerated. Those valiants of Easy Company were so dedicated to their beloved leader that they would follow him through hell. And they did. Just as the stonewall of resistance was breached, a loud explosion seemed to amplify success. The Marines charged on, undeterred by the sound. Little did they realize that their beloved leader had stepped on an antipersonnel mine.

One Easy Company corpsman and three of Jack's Marines carried Lummus to the aid station on a litter and laid him on the ground before me. Major Antonelli and some of his staff from the CP gathered nearby, horrified by the ghastly sight confronting them.

Lummus was pale from shock. His right foot had been blown away. A mangled left foot hung loosely askew from the ankle joint. Only the long shinbone, the tibia, remained of his right leg. It was attached to the femur (thighbone) above by shreds of ligaments and tendons. The flesh of the lower two-thirds of the thigh had been blown off. A long, contracted artery emerged from the remaining ragged flesh of the remainder of the thigh and lay alongside the inner aspect of those bones. Bleeding had stopped moments before, but a small pool of blood remained on the litter, marking the spot where the artery terminated. Shrapnel had destroyed his genitalia and traveled on up into his abdominal cavity. There were penetrating shrapnel wounds on the anterior surface of his abdomen. It was a detestable, repugnant, horrible, ugly, bloody, messy, sordid scene. As I knelt to start another unit of plasma, he opened his pallid eyelids, once more grinned at me, and murmured in a very weak voice, "Well, Doc, the New York Giants lost a mighty good end today."

Five hours later, on a surgery table in the Fifth Division hospital tent, he joined thousands more of his fallen comrades.

Many years later I wrote a letter of inquiry to the New York Giants. Yes, Jack had played with them for one season as an end, in 1942. He had an outstanding, sensational rookie year and was one of their most promising prospects for the future. And at the College Football Hall of Fame in South Bend, a computer spits out a tabulation of his football days of glory at Baylor University in Waco, Texas.

10

Concussion Wounds

Concussion wounds were not as common as other types of wounds in our experience at Iwo Jima. Intense waves of compressed atmosphere are generated by the explosive forces of large shells. Great quantities of energy are released. These may kill as they pass through the body by disruption of transmission of electrical currents traveling along nerve fibers of the brain or as they are transmitted across connecting junctions (synapses) of nerve endings. Massive concussive forces may disrupt brain function by instantly tearing apart or severing the axons, the long nerve fibers extending from the nucleus of one cell to another, and interrupting the electrotransmission of impulses among the millions and billions of nerve cells in the brain. Death results instantaneously when this trauma is widespread in the brain.

The tiny electrical force generated by the special cells composing the inherent pacemaker of the heart spreads through a cablelike conducting tissue to excite each muscle fiber in the heart to make all act synchronously in the hydraulic, pumping contraction of the organ. Severe concussion may also interrupt this conducting system and cause cardiac standstill and death in that organ.

Earlier I described the two columns of Japanese, one on either side of the hole in the ground caused by an exploding sixteen-inch Naval artillery shell. These indicated the instant arrest of all brain and cardiac functions, which left those men in statuelike postures. Perhaps more lines of troops spaced between those two described were blown into minuscule particles by that explosion.

Varying degrees of concussion cause varying degrees of disruption of body function. Lesser effects on the brain result in stunned or dazed sensations. Transient confusion may result and last from a few to many minutes. Loss of memory, amnesia, may leave one without recollection of any happenings from the time of an explosion until several hours or even days after the injury. Such losses may disappear gradually and memory return. However, such a loss may be permanent, with the function of memory being otherwise intact. In the episode titled "Valley of the Shadow," Leonard Nederveld had no memory of anything occurring between the time he tossed grenades into the bunker filled with large stores of ammunition and when he found himself gazing into bright daylight almost twenty hours later. Did he suffer from amnesia or unconsciousness? In his instance, it might have been either.

Leonard Therien remembers a corpsman tried to start plasma in a vein. After fifty-four years, Therien does not recall walking however far it may have been to the shell hole where he rolled on down in with his fellow Marines. He was carried by a corpsman who dumped him in the shell hole. He does not remember that because he was unconscious. He remembers the corpsman trying to start plasma on him, but fifty-four years later he still has no recall of events between that experience and when he had a return of awareness many days later in a military hospital. Personally, I think much of his memory loss of those days was and still is due to the phenomenon of amnesia due to concussion of his brain. Some men were permanently mentally deranged to some degree by concussion injuries. We witnessed none in our battalion. A very common and uncomfortable result of concussion of the brain is diffuse headache. Usually this cleared, in our experience, in a short time. Occasionally this lingers for weeks or months in individuals incurring such battle injury.

The very delicate mucosa or lining of the entire gastrointestinal tract is also extremely vulnerable to concussion forces. Concussion injury to this lining is characterized by multiple small linear tears in any part or all section of the GI tract. Blood oozes from these tears. When vomiting results from concussion, blood is part of the vomitus. Blood released into the colon or rectal pouch from such injury to that segment may be passed on out in bright red form on the stools of the injured. If the entire tract is damaged, blood may ooze from the mouth, and appear in the vomitus and in the stools as black oxidized blood and also in the bright red form. Severe pains in the abdomen result from the tears in the gut lining, as was the case with Corpsman Bill Miller of Fox Company.

Corpsman Ed Jones experienced complete but temporary deafness of very short duration as a result of the mortar shell exploding near his ear. Corpsmen Roy Brown and Lester Murrah experienced stunned feelings and numbness after being subjected to explosions strong enough to throw them up in the air. They also had dazed feelings and mild confusion, for short periods of time, indicating mild, transient derangement of function of some brain cells temporarily. They, too, had deafness, but for periods of a half hour or more. Capt. Bill King, commanding officer of Dog Company, came to the aid station because of deafness in one ear caused by the nearby explosion of a mortar shell. Examination of the affected ear revealed fresh bleeding due to the traumatic rupture of the eardrum. In his case, a longer recovery time of three months was noted.

Occasionally tears in the lining of the bladder may cause bleeding when they occur as a result of nearby strong explosive forces. None were witnessed in our aid station.

11

Miscellaneous

Foxhole Buddies

The primary duty of a combat corpsman assigned to our rifle companies was to do all that he could for the wounded at the front. Occasionally he would hold in his arms a dying man of his own platoon, in a meager attempt to bring comfort to a wounded soldier Sometimes he treated men of other battalions who happened to meet misfortune and crossed into our area This type of misdirection was more likely when situations were very fluid and confusion reigned in the smoke and dust of intense activity. When caring for others, the corpsmen were typically too busy with their primary obligations to the wounded to attempt to defend themselves. Sometimes they had to, and did. Bill Miller was corpsman of Fox Company, who ran about with abandon on the battlefield caring for the wounded.

Once he recounted to me a gut-wrenching experience of a quiet moment. The silence of the nocturnal watch he was keeping in his foxhole was broken by intermittent variable sounds, which seemed to him like the noise of someone crawling around out there, some enemy perhaps attempting to infiltrate the lines in the darkness. Nothing was visible. He pulled his K-bar from its sheath in preparedness and waited. The sound seemed to be inching closer. The darkness of the night made it difficult for him to see and to decipher the direction of the sound impossible. All at once, something hit him hard in the back, so hard that it knocked the breath out of him. So hard that he dropped his K-bar. A Japanese had surprised him from the rear. He quickly recovered from the surprise.

"I didn't want to kill anyone," Bill later told me. "But it was either him or me. I struggled for all I was worth. He was a lot smaller than I, and finally I succeeded in getting my arm around his neck and squeezed it as hard as I could. Finally he collapsed. I held on for a minute or two—scared and alone. Happily I survived, I felt bad because he was someone's son or brother or husband.

"The next time, killing didn't bother me as much. Early one morning our platoon caught a lot of mortar fire. On checking one man who had fallen at my right, I found him dead, killed instantly. I jumped into a crowded foxhole ahead of me for shelter. I looked about to see if any men in there were wounded. One man tried wiggling out from under the dead body of another. One arm was pinned to the ground by the corpse, and in the other hand he still held a pistol. Suddenly I realized he wore a Japanese gray uniform, his own; he also wore the nonmatching helmet of a U.S. Marine. In the chaos, none of the Marines had yet detected the infiltration.

"Just then Corporal Bolger walked up to the edge of the foxhole. As he knelt down, he was hit by rifle fire and fell over into the foxhole, partially lying across me. I pulled a battle dressing from my kit to dress his wounded shoulder just as he took a direct hit from one of those mortar shells. It ripped his torso terribly, and also killed the two live Marines who were in there with me. I looked at the Japanese, but he appeared to be dead, too. A fierce, hard pain filled my entire abdomen. Just then the Jap began to move and pull free. Crawling out from under Bolger's body, and up over the edge of the hole, I went for my carbine. It was there on the ground, about twenty feet from the foxhole. I pushed off the safety and headed back to the foxhole. As I returned, I dropped to the ground and cautiously crawled around in a wide semicircle to the side opposite the back of that man with the pistol. Sure enough, he was there peeping over the opposite edge with his pistol ready, looking in the direction of my departure. He heard me coming and began to turn. I shot him in the head before he could get me."

While walking back from the front two days later, a weakened Miller collapsed. Litter bearers brought him the rest of the way. He reported that he vomited blood and passed blood from his bowels. Indeed, he was very weak and pale. We checked him, especially his abdomen, and told him his stomach and bowel were injured by the concussion. We started plasma intravenously and shipped him back to a hospital. He was transferred to a ship. Subsequently he returned to our battalion at Camp Tarawa. The concussion produced tears in the lining of the bowel and stomach, which resulted in the bleeding.

Many months later when we were in Japan, he began having trouble with the abdominal pains again. He was shipped back to a U.S. Navy hospital in California, where X rays revealed an ulcer in his stomach. Doctors there had told him it might be related to the concussion injury.

Tortured

What his name was or outfit was, was not known to us. He was a member of another and adjacent battalion or regiment. He vanished in unspectacular fashion from among his comrades. The cause and nature of his disappearance were unknown.

A few days later his fellow Marines over ran the enemy forces. As they "mopped up" the area they found his nude body suspended by the ankles from the roof of one of those innumerable caves. The free end of his tongue was cut away. A pile of cigarette butts lay on the floor below his head and was mute testimony of the cruelty of his captors. The skin of every part of his body was mutilated by a variety of burns caused by cigarettes pressed against it. Some of the burns were large; some were small. Some were deep; some were shallow. They all manifested the hideous, evil, cruel behavior of enemy soldiers as they burned and mocked and jeered him in his dying hours.

There were no consoling words and voices in those final moments; no old friends, no bereaved loved ones to cover him with endearments as he passed into eternity. No comforts of home or of a hospital eased his dying. All those were thousands of miles away. His was an ignominious flight from life marked by the degrading behavior of degenerate torturers. What wicked, diabolic, corrupt savages they were to mock and shriek derisively and continually torture him in those fatal hours—and, oh, so very far away from home.

Only the corrupt and bestial would behave so savagely and torture their fellow men in that brutal manner. How typical it was of the infamous behavior of certain groups of the enemy. Such acts by members of the Japanese Army did not necessarily shock the conscience of the ruling military elite or of the Japanese society itself in the years they were winning in Manchuria and along the north China coast.

My Dirty Uniform

Corpsman Lester Murrah related this anecdote, which is a vivid reflection of an ugliness, one of many, that was part of daily routine for corpsmen who served with frontline rifle companies:

The battle was several days old. I had dealt with numerous wounds to that point. Major Antonelli came forward to our Easy Company command post. He was probably checking out the strength of the outfit, or its strategic situation, or perhaps he was laying out instructions for our next move. From time to time we corpsmen were very busy caring for the wounded. My dungarees were saturated with blood, and bits of flesh had been smeared or pressed against

152

those clothes as I had carried or lifted or turned the wounded in caring for their wounds. I had also gotten soiled from pulling the men into foxholes or back to our platoon area where they had fallen in the front lines. We hadn't been able to wash for days because of danger and intense action. My dungarees stank because of the old, dried blood and the rotting flesh which tainted them. The Major was standing but a very few feet from me talking to one of the company officers. All at once he turned suddenly and pointed at me saying, "Get that man a clean uniform. He smells terrible."

He had smelled the stinking old blood and flesh and had recognized their odors. It was so very kind of him to take notice of and care for such a little disagreeable, uncomfortable situation when he was occupied with things of much more importance. That situation revealed to me his sincere consideration for each individual fighting in his command and his concern for every one of them.

Mistaken Identity

Litter bearers did not train with us on field maneuvers. They were transferred from replacement battalions. Attached to their respective assault units shortly before they shipped out from Hawaii, they had little actual training for battle action. Late one evening of the battle, a call came for the evacuation of a wounded man from the front lines. Four litter bearers responded and headed forward to retrieve the injured Marine. He received emergency treatment on the spot from the platoon corpsman. One of the litter bearers was a Navajo Indian by ancestry. He must have been of minimal acceptable stature, as mandated by the USMC, when he enlisted.

The litter bearers soon arrived at the platoon area, to which the subject of their retrieval was removed. By this time daylight was gone. As they lifted the wounded man to the litter, they realized their crew was short one man, the Navajo. He had disappeared during the trip forward. No one saw him after they left the company headquarters area.

The impaired Marine on the litter was transported to our aid station for further care of his wounds and for recording. A few minutes later an amphibious tractor, in use as an ambulance on its final mission of the day, pulled up alongside the aid station to load any other casualties for transport back to the division hospital. A few ambulatory wounded were sitting on the deck of the LVT. Two litter patients were also aboard. One of the aid station corpsmen noted an unusual occupant within the vehicle handcuffed to two armed Marine guards and standing against the bulwark of the opposite side. Using a flashlight, the corpsman recognized the Navajo litter bearer who became lost in the darkness as his team ran forward. He had wandered into territory occupied by another battalion. There, in the darkness, he was apprehended by personnel of that battalion who assumed him to be one of the enemy infiltrating in the night. Fortunately no one fired on him. He was released on the spot and escorted back to the base of his operation. All's well that ends well.

The Spy

In the midafternoon of a cloudy fifteenth day of battle, we in the aid station could hear the sharp cracks of rifles firing, the noisy clatter of lesser machine guns, and the splatting sounds of small mortar shells exploding at the front, a couple hundred yards ahead. These were sounds of a moderately intense firefight, and already we were occupied with caring for nonlethal wounds of three of our own casualties. As for myself, my focus was absorbed in the suturing of a jagged six-inch-long shrapnel wound in the lateral aspect of the left thigh of a comrade Marine. He lay at full length on the litter by which he had been carried into our full-disclosure aid station. The word *absorbed* is used because it was necessary to meticulously appose the irregular shaggy edges of the skin into exact alignment with one another. The wound was a shallow one, involving just the skin and underlying layer of fatty tissue. No muscle tissue was damaged. Since haste was not a priority, I desired to do the task as well as possible, so it would not be necessary to cut all the sutures apart and start all over in a rear-echelon hospital.

The nearby scuffing sound of footwear against rocks disrupted my attention. Out of the corner of my left eye, a vague figure of one as tall as I was approaching. As I paused to turn in response, my attention changed; a Japanese soldier wearing a conical straw hat, such as some of the enemy troops wore, entered. His gray Japanese Army uniform was devoid of any insignias. Some of the "old salts" from the Solomon battles had related to me tales they had heard of Nisei men being used to infiltrate enemy lines and collect intelligence. Obviously he was one of those returning from such a venture. He then asked in unaccented, clear-cut English, "Where is the regimental command post?"

That convinced me of the accuracy of my conclusion. In a perfunctory, not very explicit gesture, while pointing the needle holder in my right hand grip to some farther direction in the rear, I answered, "Back that way somewhere." The whole episode took not more than one or two minutes. He was already headed back to report to regimental intelligence. I might have been delayed by the time required for inserting three or four more sutures in the wound beneath; only a blip of attention was drawn from this repair job.

The following morning some personage from regimental headquarters came on some kind of mission to our Second Battalion CP. He mentioned, incidentally, that a Japanese colonel had surrendered himself to our regimental CO, Tom Wornham, the afternoon before. The man had been educated at Oxford University in England and spoke perfect English. The rest of his story was to the effect that he had had his bellyful of war. He discerned that the Japanese were losing the battle for Iwo, and he saw no point in dying needlessly for their emperor in a lost cause.

So much for my *bleep* conclusions.

12

Wounds of the Mind and Spirit

The Yellow Bird

The stresses of battle, including tremendous explosions, bloody horrors, loss of dear friends, uncertainties of blackest darkness at night, and incessant exposure to weapons fire, these and a host of other traumatizing factors, precipitate dysfunctions of the human minds. These dysfunctions may be transient or may be permanent. Corpsman Lester Murrah of 2-27 (Easy Company-Second Battalion-Twenty-seventh Regiment) experienced a delusional plague that endured throughout the battle, yet it did not impair any functions or abilities.

It began shortly after he hit the beach in the nature of a small yellow bird flying about wherever he went, day and night. Sharp, loud noises that one would expect to alarm birds had no effect on Murrah's avian acquaintance. He threw stones at it without inflicting harm or fright. Its peculiar call was constantly informing the enemy of his whereabouts. He did not understand why, with that signal at their disposal, the enemy could not hit him with some kind of missile. He grew used to it and ignored it. He at last acknowledged to himself that it wasn't really there even though it was very apparent.

Like a furtive little sibling, it persisted in trailing along, popping up anywhere and anytime when least expected. And just as unexpectedly, at the end of battle it vanished forever.

Combat Fatigue

In World War I the condition was labeled shellshock. In World War II we called it combat fatigue, different nomenclature for the same clinical condition. It has been mistakenly interpreted as an indication of cowardice. Believe me, it isn't. Under the strain of frequent bombardment, machine-gun fire, and incessantly exploding grenades, some soldiers endured all they could take emotionally. Sometimes the sudden death of a nearby buddy or comrade was the last straw for these patriots. Those stresses caused a few men to temporarily disintegrate emotionally and mentally. Men with the problem blubbered incoherently or cried uncontrollably when brought into the aid station from the front. Some tried to break loose and return to the front. These men we were obliged to strap to stretchers with belts and wide-band adhesive tape. At the front lines some men with this condition dashed toward the enemy with disorganized reason. Sometimes they were killed; sometimes they were caught by others and returned to safety and on to the rear of the action.

Actually, victims of combat fatigue were few in number. Some were stoic veterans of other battles. For others, it occurred in this, their first combat experience. We all felt the strain. Fortunately, most contained and handled the stresses of Iwo Jima. Outwardly or inwardly, the stress of constant apprehension, terror, horror, mutilation, or fiery death left every one of us uptight. One of our corpsmen remarked that of all the men he observed in battle, I was the most composed. But in the winter of 1949, years after the battle, a surprising delayed reaction of combat fatigue suddenly gripped me. It was illustrative of the more subtle, indelible marks combat left in the psychological depths of many a soldier.

This incident occurred during the last year of my residency in internal medicine. Every third night we residents were on call. Sometimes nothing time-consuming happened during such calls. Other such nights brimmed with constant activity. In one particular stretch of work, after I reported in at 7:00 A.M., a busy schedule occupied me all day. The ensuing night was filled with one emergency after another. The following day was also a very busy one until 7:00 P.M. It seemed to me to be one of ceaseless physical and mental drudgery. Like the weary plowman, I wended my way homeward, arriving wholly exhausted forty minutes later.

Upon my arrival at our home, my wife began preparation for a late-evening dinner. I turned on the radio and stretched my full length on the sofa in hope of relaxing for just a few minutes prior to terminating what seemed to be a long, long period of starvation—eight hours. I turned on the radio, and the announcer informed the listening audience, "Tonight we bring you *Columbia Was There,*" one of a then-current broadcast series of historic events recalled by recitation and by sound in simulation of the real moment. William L. Shirer, or someone of equal descriptive talent, continued, "Tonight, ladies and gentlemen, we bring alive that momentous event: the invasion of Normandy Beach."

The program must have been supported with real soundtracks of the actual assault. Dive bombers screamed downward. Their bombs exploded with horrendous force. Shells from those mammoth battleships out at sea screeched overhead. Bullets hissed for a bit of a second as they zipped by. Large mortar shells burst with terrific force a short distance away. All at once I, too, disintegrated emotionally. After shivering and crying uncontrollably for a few minutes, I pointed to the radio and pleaded, "Turn it off! Please. Turn it off!" My frightened but composed wife hurried to my side at that unexpected reaction.

She complied, and in ten minutes that frightening reaction passed. The combination of physical and mental fatigue, plus low blood sugar, and the striking of some long-since-hidden chords in the mental grooves of my structured emotion, whatever that may be, undid me. How amazing that the wonderful composure that had sustained me in the heat of battle was destroyed so instantly by a group of innocent forces acting in unexpected instant unison years later.

Even to this day, the *Purple Heart* is awarded for physical wounds that merit citation. Yet the terrors, anguish, fears, losses, horrible sights of human destruction in battle are just as disfiguring, just as maiming, just as distorting, and sometimes just as permanent in the mind as the physical injuries may be. The nerve-racking battle dreams, those cold sweats, and shaking may go on for years before they disappear. Sometimes they continue until the very end of life. Sometimes they recur indefinitely because their scars are in the nature of disinterred, sequestered, long-entombed memories that—in the middle of nocturnal rest—electrify a small collection of cells that ordinarily suppress those residual visions. No, there is no bleeding, no ripping of flesh, no shattering of bones. The wounds aren't visible, yet oftentimes they are indeed as painful as visible wounds.

A Letter from Home

Corporal Kristner (not his real name) was a good Marine. His records were clear: he was a leader and an achiever. Yet he did not appear to be aggressive. He was cooperative, obedient, neat, and cheerful. He understood his duties, which he fulfilled well. When given orders, he executed them promptly. He was well liked by all of Fox Company.

Two or three weeks before we shipped out from Camp Tarawa for battle, drastic personality changes came over Kristner. He withdrew from his common, daily associations in many respects and became a loner. He did not talk much to anyone and apparently preferred not to. In the bit I wrote about crossing the island after hitting the beach, I mentioned encountering Lt. Don Hendricks leaning against a tree and that he told me the Second Platoon was pinned down fifty or sixty feet up ahead by a large

Nambu (or heavy Japanese machine gun) and was unable to move forward. Corporal Kristner was in that platoon. The story does not end there. One evening after chow as we sailed back to Pearl Harbor aboard the *USS Storm King,* Chief Ph M Milt Klinger and myself were standing at the leeward rail recounting a few memorable incidents of the battle. I mentioned that particular one, because it occurred in the first hour or two of the conflict. A member of Fox Company told me previously of his being stopped like all the others and lying immobile on the ground for what seemed a long time because of that troublesome Nambu. Whenever anyone stirred just a bit, the machine gun fired into action and blasted away at them. A couple of guys were wounded, but not badly. They were unable to evacuate them under the fierce fire. No one could spot the location of the weapon causing all the trouble, so well was it camouflaged. They were absolutely stymied for at least one half hour. Suddenly Kristner stood upright, pointing and yelling, "There it is!" He was immediately felled by a hail of machine-gun bullets. The same raconteur told me that on one occasion a few weeks before we left camp Kristner had received a letter from someone back home. He did not say who wrote it. Immediately afterward, Kristner became very morose and unsociable and lost his appetite. A few days later, the man asked Kristner why the sudden change in behavior. Kristner confided that the letter bore information about his wife chasing around back home.

Milt finally broke a lengthy pause in our conversation. "You know, Doctor, that was a helluva thing to do, sending that letter. It was worse than bad taste. Here we were. All of us were uptight about going into battle and not knowing whether we would come out of it alive or badly impaired or killed. Possibly that knowledge about his wife made him so dejected and indifferent about survival he had no compunction about sacrificing himself. On the other hand, he was the sort of a chap who would readily do whatever was necessary to rescue the others from such grave jeopardy. We'll never know, will we?"

Lougee and the Dying

Ph M 1/C Glenn Lougee was in charge of Fox Company's corpsmen in combat. Corpsmen were constantly subjected to the worst of battle experiences. The ever-unexpected, changing circumstances gave rise to a high degree of anxiety, desperation and helplessness. "I saw such devastation," Lougee recalls. Once he observed wounded carrying other, more severely wounded from the battle scene. Anxiety resulted from knowing that lives were saved or lost if the immediate and proper treatment could not be given in time. Often anxiety quickly grabbed one as he left the protection of his foxhole during a rain of explosions to treat the very wounds they had caused. Lougee told me, in a moment of reverie fifty years after the fact, that he sometimes held mortally wounded men in his arms during their dying moments. Helplessness at such times took on a new meaning in battle, the frustration of helplessness of comforting the dying. Several times dying men requested, "You tell them for me, . . ." and expired before completing the thought that possessed their minds. Each one of those men looked up into Lougee's eyes and pleaded, "You will tell them, won't you?"

Tell whom? Tell them what? The enigma perturbed him over and over. He pondered for an explanation, for none clarified the mysterious dying wish. Sufficient life did not remain. Something one such man said finally implied the answer. In his last breath he whispered, "Tell them back home that I died fighting—fighting for my country and for all those I love. You will tell them, won't you?"

No, we haven't forgotten you or what you did for our country. Indeed, what you did for the entire free world. Thank you for making the ultimate sacrifice.

Victory without Wings

As we sailed west for Kwajalein toward Saipan aboard the *USS Highlands,* we were administered a briefing, one afternoon, by the Intelligence Section of our battalion. We learned that our target had been bombed steadily by our air forces for two months and that it would be shelled by the big sixteen-inch guns of our battleships for three days prior to D-Day. That tremendous pounding with explosives would inflict such harm (so intelligence thought) that the battle would be short-lived: three days maximum. Three or four more days would be needed to "mop up" afterward. We would then board ship and head on to Guam to train in preparation for the next operation. Intelligence did not know about the twenty-five miles of tunnels on Iwo Jima and all their ramifications.

When action began on D-Day, 21,000 Sons of the Rising Sun stayed staunchly in place, dedicated to dying for their "divine" emperor. They stoically awaited the 30,000 U.S. Marines who came ashore that first day. In the days that followed, reinforced by naval gunfire and later tanks as well, the Marine infantry plowed slowly forward toward its objectives. The Twenty-eighth Regiment of the Fifth Division landed on Green Beach One near Mt. Suribachi. The Second Battalion, Twenty-seventh, landed on Red Beach One, on the right flank of the Twenty-eighth and the left of the First Battalion on Red Beach Two. The Fourth Division's battalions landed on the right flank of the Fifth on Yellow Beaches One and Two and Blue Beaches One and Two. Each of these beaches was five hundred feet wide in the battle plan, and they sequentially ranged the east coast of Iwo from Suribachi to the cliffs along the Boat Basin thirty-five hundred feet to the north. They were in a real meat grinder. The enemy was firing all kinds of ammunition at the Marines from positions above on Mt. Suribachi. From the high ground to the north they showered the works at the Marines from the opposite direction. Casualties were so high on

D-Day that elements of the floating reserve, the Third Marine Division, were ordered to land late in the afternoon. Every minute of daylight for the first three weeks, our troops were faced with wounding and death from unseen snipers, camouflaged spider traps and bunkers, and mortar, artillery, and rocket barrages based on the high ground at the north standing well above them. Hours of darkness were filled with nightmares of war. Random rounds of mortar and artillery shells exploded nearby. Silent infiltrators slithered among our foxholes looking for opportunities to jump in, shoot, and stab. Surprise banzai attacks screamed out of nowhere.

For a few glorious moments during the morning of the fifth day of the conflict our forces were inspired by the unexpected sight of our nation's ensign unfurled in the bright sunshine and rippling in a strong breeze above Suribachi. A mighty cheer went up among all of our troops on the island and among those supporting forces manning the great flotilla out at sea. No longer was that part of the enemy south of our lines putting us in the uncomfortable position of being caught in crossfire from both the front and the rear. We enjoyed a sense of victory ahead, not really realizing how distant it was. Turning once more to the task before us, we little perceived the magnitude and the duration of what lay ahead for us.

Finally, the casualties among the Marines began to decrease as the mortality numbers mounted among the Japanese. There were no reserves, no replacements, for that enemy dedicated to dying for its "divine emperor." In the latter days of battle, when the Marines were supposedly "mopping up," killing and still being killed among the deep gorges, great rocks, many caves, and high cliffs at the north end of the island, our men at the front were able to withdraw at night to the safety of their company command areas, sleep, and return to the search for the hidden enemy in the morning.

Early in the afternoon of the thirty-sixth day, without any cheering or smiles or celebration, we ceased fighting on order. The United States had been victorious. Only a meager remnant of our battalion remained. Of Dog Company's original 240 men, 65 answered muster; of Easy, 35; and of Fox, 25. Fewer casualties were experienced in the much-smaller Headquarters Company. Of our original battalion roster of 850, 137 were killed in battle. A few more of the original number died in hospitals elsewhere, and 450 more were wounded. Those of us still able-bodied fell into formation and marched in file, two by two, quietly, sullenly, to the rear of the island toward Suribachi and the black sand beaches where we landed on D-Day. Just beyond the south end of Airfield #1 the narrow column filed right and marched on just past the gate of the Fifth Marine Division Cemetery. There it stopped on the order "Halt." The men then turned ninety degrees to the left, and at the order to be at rest the troops broke ranks and headed into the cemetery to look for markers denoting the sites where cherished comrades rested below in death.

After a substantial period of heart-tugging, unrestrained tears and grieving, we fell into formation once more and marched on farther to the western beach just opposite the east coast and the deep black sands of the Red Beaches where our assault began ages ago on February 19, 1945. We cleaned and checked our weapons. We turned in our live ammunition as ordered. We weren't interested in firing those weapons anymore. Some sat smoking cigarettes and conversing in low tones. Others simply sat in placid, quiet contemplation of the past thirty-six days or, better yet, of home. Each of us was acutely aware of that. The next time around who would be killed? The man on either side of me or all three of us? There was no air of jubilation, no champagne. Later that day we marched up the gangplank of the USS *Storm King* along with the rest of the tatters of the Twenty-seventh Marines. The piercing thought struck home that on the outbound voyage preceding battle each of the three battalions plus support troops occupied a similar entire troopship. Once aboard, we each received a new outfit of dungarees. We cleansed our dirty bodies in hot showers, donned the clean clothes, ate decent, warm chow, and set sail on the return trip eastward back to Hawaii and Camp Tarawa.

Accompanying the Marines in the first wave and the next several thereafter in that struggle on Iwo was a very small, incorporated group of young men trained not to wound, maim, and kill an enemy but to salvage insofar as possible, the bodies and lives of our wounded and to assist those who were hopelessly dying. It consisted of litter bearers, corpsmen, and medical doctors. These men lived among the Marines in training, sharing joys, sorrows, apprehensions, discomforts, pictures and goodies from home, and stories of loves left behind and of the best of Marine grub, Spam and deluxe, reconstituted, dried, scrambled eggs—the best Uncle Sam could afford. We in that smaller force trained alongside our buddies the Marines. We learned to use K-bars, bayonets, pistols, carbines, M-1s, rifles, and grenades. We learned to "snoop and poop" and to find such shelter as might serve in self-preservation. We also trained to help and treat medically, not to harm. In the heat, smoke, and clamor of battle we cast aside our arms and self-concerns to execute those duties assigned to us in particular, that is, to treat and rescue casualties on the front lines, to see that the casualties were transported back to the aid station, if need be, or minister to them on the spot and send them back to duty again. Often casualties were transported directly to station hospitals well behind us. We lived very closely with one another and with our fellow Marines throughout those exciting, horrifying, tragic thirty-six days. We shared danger, sad moments, and death. Five of our litter bearers and six of our corpsmen were killed in battle. When we sailed away from the island, part of my body, part of my spirit, and part of my soul remained on Iwo Jima.

One of my little rewards, more precious than citations and medals came years later at the 1985 reunion of the Fifth Marine Division Association on Long Island. One of those salty old warriors, who had averaged nineteen years of age at the time of the assault, approached me with an extended hand exclaiming, "Doctor, I want to shake your hand and thank you for saving my life back there on Iwo forty years ago!"

13

The Last and the Deepest

The day was a long one in my very active practice of internal medicine. It continued well into that late-summer night of 1989. Eleven o'clock had just passed as I returned from work at Ball Memorial Hospital. Sheer fatigue flooded through me as I walked through the family room and sat to relax at the end of a trying day. Others of the family were asleep. Reading, snacking, watching TV, or listening to classical music did not appeal. My intent was to sit in untroubled serenity a few minutes until the sensations of tension and fatigue cleared and then move on upstairs to bed. The buzzing, pushing, intense feelings within needed to subside after fifteen hours of persistent work had reduced me to a worthless lump of human putty.

The telephone rang. NOT AGAIN! That evil device, very necessary among the aids to making my livelihood, dared me, challenged, me taunted me, beckoned me to action once more when it was almost impossible to respond to its spiteful ring. Why, why, why was I inspired those many years ago to go to medical school? Dutifully I dragged my aching feet and legs and heart across the room to answer, muttering hatefully as I went. What nocturnal needs troubled some diseased fellowman to impose on me from the other end of that wicked conduit of communication? I could only speculate in dreariness.

"Dr. Brown, this is Ed Jones calling from Seattle. Remember me? . . . For the past couple of years I've often thought of calling you, but never did. This time I did it. I had no idea whether you still lived in Muncie, or, for that matter, whether you might yet be alive. It has been forty-four years. I finally decided to chance it. The information operator in Muncie must know you. When I inquired, she said she would connect me with your home and immediately did. Do you remember when we parted for our homes there at Camp Pendleton?"

Remember? How could one forget? He was like a kid brother then. All of them were. It returned so vividly. There must have been ten or twelve of my corpsmen in that canopied six-by-six. They sat on the benches on either side of that late-model Conestoga. The combat fatigues had been traded for new, green, flannel, dress-type greens. They joked, shook my hand, and exchanged addresses with me as they waited. They were a happy little group of battle-weathered young men, old before their time. After seventeen long months overseas, including thirty-six days of battle on Iwo Jima, the long, melancholy voyage back to Hawaii, four months more training for another assault, and three months' occupation duty at Saga, Kyushu, Japan, instead, beginning the last leg of a long journey home was a godsend.

Remember? You bet I did. We talked on and on for forty minutes. The very firm bond developed by those horrible thirty-six days shared at Iwo Jima lasted all through those intervening years to go on forever. We were all part of the medical section of Headquarters Company, Second Battalion, Twenty-seventh Marines. We managed and served in its Sick Bay at Camp Pendleton and Camp Tarawa. We lived and trained with those Marines, our buddies, for one year before the great battle. We immunized them, treated their bad colds and sore feet, shared tents, powdered eggs, old movies, and training maneuvers. We patched them together and watched them shed blood and watched some of them die for their nation as they succumbed to the wounds of war. Six of our corpsmen were among the 137 left behind on Iwo. One or two wounded returned to our unit at Camp Tarawa after recovering from wounds at Aiea Heights Hospital near Pearl Harbor. More recovered after long periods of convalescence at U.S. Navy base hospitals in the States. Forget? Never.

We talked on and on. Ed had graduated from the University of Washington in Seattle. He majored in accounting. Early on in his career he had invested in a downtown Seattle parking garage. After a number of years he sold it and bought a second and larger one. It was replaced by a third and even much larger one than the second. In the meantime, the son born to us (my wife and myself) while I was engaged in battle was joined by seven more siblings to fill the quiver. By this time in the call my fatigue was replaced by the delight of the renewal of our acquaintance.

Finally Ed said, "Dr. Brown, I thought you were the most composed of all the men I observed throughout that battle. You appeared unruffled throughout all that action. Do you recall the morning at Pendleton when we corpsmen climbed into that truck to go to the railroad station in Los Angeles and on to our various homes from there?

"I recall you standing there on the tarvia behind that truck parked by the office. Some of us were talking happily and laughing. Some of us jotted down your home address. After ten minutes, the driver revved up the motor and all the chatter stopped. You stood there alone on the pavement waving to us. All at once tears streamed down both your cheeks. As the truck slowly rolled forward, I started crying. I couldn't help it. Then all the other fellows on the truck started crying. That went on for several minutes. Then it stopped. The rest of that ride was pretty quiet."

During that long-winded conversation, I told Ed about the Fifth Marine Division Association and its annual reunions.

"Do many of our corpsmen attend?"

"A few."

"Good. I'll see you in San Diego next year." He was there. So were Jerry Cunningham and Roy Brown and Bill Miller and Paul Bradford and Carl Schraiber, all good men and true.

168

Epilogue

A few months ago a letter of inquiry was sent to the more respon-
sive surviving corpsmen of our battalion. They were once young
men, part of a group who loved their buddies and attended them as
they fought and bled and sometimes died. The question was:
"What effects did your experiences in the battle at Iwo Jima have
on your life thereafter?" Their responses varied in character and
length.

Ed Jones's reply was simplest. It expressed his thankfulness
that he was young enough and naive enough at the time that he experienced no mental trauma and did not absorb all the horrors to
the extent that he was bothered with wild battle dreams and cold
sweats at night. He remained psychologically stable. As soon as
feasible he enrolled at the University of Washington in Seattle,
pursuing an accounting major. One battle scene remains indelibly
imprinted in his mind, that of Lt. Jack Lummus as he was carried
from the front into our aid station on a stretcher after he stepped on
an antipersonnel mine. Jones watched the whole scene and saw the
extensive wounds: "His legs were like toothpicks. . . ."

Lester Murrah related that he was far more mature for his age
when he returned home because of his battle experiences. He had
acquired a sense of discipline. If something needed to be done, he
did it right now, without procrastinating. Some of the terrifying
experiences bothered him, nightmares accompanied by cold
sweats. He sought employment after he was discharged from the
USN and as soon as he returned home. He found work interesting
to him and made a career of it. The challenges of his work mini-

mized the emotional distresses resulting from the battle. He is even yet disturbed by memories of the horrors of war. He avoids discussing some of those experiences with former Marine comrades and refuses to read of them.

Paul Bradford:

As to how the battle experiences affected my life, I am unsure other than to look at how I seemed to be prior to the battle as contrasted with what I was at the time of my discharge from the service. I aged/matured a lot as a result.

I often think of the hell it was on Iwo Jima, and of those who did not survive. How thankful I am I came through it. The first couple of years (as a civilian) I used to awaken at night in a sweat recalling how it was. Occasionally I picked small pieces of shrapnel from my thigh. All that has passed. I'm glad to have endured a long and happy life, and a still enduring marriage of fifty-four years.

Remember when you did my pre-marital physical and blood tests for my bride-to-be and self at Glenview Naval Air Station when you were still on active duty there? You know my children, Steve and Sally. They have been real joys and inspirations. They helped me forget it a lot.

Glen Lougee:

Having been subjected to the unceasing and varied and extreme stresses of battle, it utterly surprised me that I never lost my cool. I came to know, through daily experiences, the extremes of fear, desperation, helplessness, and grief. I concluded myself to be stronger mentally and possessing a physical endurance beyond my pre-battle concept. This inspired a new confidence in myself as well as the knowledge I can meet any challenge civilian life ever presents.

Battle brought out the essentials of life, emphasizing the importance of the *do it now* attitude, before it is too late; that is, to offer the gifts of praise and inspiration to those most dear before beneficial time runs out. The application of this philosophy has blessed me with no regrets.

The main influence of the battle experience to me was my vocational choice. Being daily aware I lived because others had died, directly or indirectly, I felt an obligation to give myself to something of lasting value. At the time, I was working in production in TV in New York. Who could ask for a better opportunity? The spirit of Semper Fidelis was still with me. I decided to give my life to kids, the future of this country, the country for which those men died. I became a high school biology teacher at a time when teachers were needed.

Now retired, I bask in the gratitude of those I whom I successfully encouraged and inspired to be all they could be. After thirty years, I still hear and follow their successes. I am still active with youth in my church and neighborhood. The battle experience taught me people are more important than things. The complete joy and happiness they have given me has fulfilled my life beyond measure.

Two examples stand out in my mind. The first involved four biology students who, with me, planned and prepared in detail a surgical splenectomy on a live rat. This we did one Saturday morning in our high school biology laboratory. The operation was a surgical success. The rat survived. Better yet, the four students later entered medical school. The second: Imagine attending two symphony concerts in Carnegie Hall, New York, directed by another of my students. I am at peace now. I have been faithful to those gallant Marines, my students, and to myself.

THE END

Bibliography

Closing In, Col. Robert Alexander, USMC.

Encyclopedia Britannica, Vol. X, 79, "History of Japan."

Iwo Jima, Richard Newcombe, Holt, Rinehart & Winston, Medal of Honor, 305, Lummus.